WE HAVE SEEN THE LORD!

We Have Seen the Lord!

The Passion and Resurrection of Jesus Christ

WILLIAM BARCLAY

Westminster John Knox Press
Louisville, Kentucky

Book design by Sharon Adams
Cover design by Jennifer Cox
Cover photograph by © 1998 PhotoDisc, Inc.

First Edition
Published by Westminster John Knox Press
Louisville, Kentucky

This book is printed on acid-free paper that meets
the American National Standards Institute Z39.48 standard. ∞

PRINTED IN THE UNITED STATES OF AMERICA
99 00 01 02 03 04 05 06 07 — 10 9 8 7 6 5 4 3 2

Library of Congress Cataloging-in-Publication Data

Barclay, William, 1907–1978.
    We have seen the Lord! : the passion and Resurrection of Jesus
Christ / William Barclay.
        p.   cm.
    ISBN 0-664-25807-7
    1. Jesus Christ—Passion—Meditations.   2. Lent—Meditations.
I. Title
BT431.B26   1998
223.96—dc21   98-35961

Contents

Preface

William Barclay's Daily Study Bible—New Testament has been one of the world's most popular commentaries since he first wrote articles on portions of Mark and Luke for the *Life and Work* magazine of the Church of Scotland fifty years ago. In his commentaries, which grew to become a seventeen-volume series, Barclay has explored the New Testament book by book, section by section, sometimes verse by verse, and occasionally word by word. Each major unit is introduced with his own translation from the Greek text. The depth and range of his research not only supports his thorough exposition of scripture but also often provides a detailed and fascinating look at life in New Testament times.

This book is a reader for Lent—including daily readings from scripture that lead up to and tell the Easter story, with Barclay's writings excerpted from the Daily Study Bible for each reading. It is structured to provide a basis for a daily Lenten discipline for those who wish to use it in that way. Every attempt has been made to keep the daily readings short enough to be practical, yet full enough to give a satisfying completeness to each day's reading.

In a book of this nature, much more must be left out than may be put in. However, we hope that these readings will provide you both inspiration and information and, if they whet your appetite, aim you toward the readily available volumes of the Daily Study Bible.

As it is said of scripture, so may it be said of the Daily Study Bible and of these excerpts from it: "Jesus did many other signs in the presence of his disciples which have not been written in this book. These have been written that you may believe that Jesus is the Anointed One, the Son of God, and that believing you may have life in his name!" (John 20:31).

Walt Sutton

Introduction

The four Gospels differ widely in the ways they begin their stories about the life of Jesus. Matthew carefully establishes Jesus' royal lineage; Mark quickly identifies him as One whose coming was long-promised through the prophets; Luke tells of his humble but divinely blessed birth; John sings poetically about the incarnation of the Word through which God establishes all things. The Gospel writers are unanimous, though, in their insistence that Jesus' life reveals both the presence of God among us and the essence of humanity.

The Gospel accounts differ and agree in other ways too. Matthew, Mark, and Luke share many stories and sayings, and tend to follow a common timeline for Jesus' ministry. The Gospel of John follows a different timeline, includes material not found in the other three, and omits some matters to which they give considerable significance. Despite those differences, the four agree strongly on at least three points.

They each recognize that Jesus spent considerable time and effort teaching his disciples about who he was, and about what their discipleship would require of them.

All four also are clear that Jesus' actions and teaching brought him into escalating conflict with the religious authorities, conflict that ultimately led them to crucify him.

Finally, the four agree that Death could not hold him. When the powers of the world had done their utmost, even that was not enough. "He is risen," chorus the four Gospels.

The readings that follow are drawn from Barclay's writings about the Gospels, from sections that bear upon Jesus' identity, his teaching, his death, and his resurrection.

To think about Easter, we need to give attention to each of these areas of emphasis. Jesus becomes fully understandable only against the background of his people's messianic expectations, and of his teachings about God's Kingdom. In that light, these strands become woven into one story that rises through hope, learning, confrontations, isolation, and despair, to the rising shout of the Gospels: "He is risen!"

"He is risen," sing back the faithful. "He is risen indeed!"

Walt Sutton

Ash Wednesday

John 1:1–18

When the world had its beginning, the Word was already there; and the Word was with God; and the Word was God. This Word was in the beginning with God. He was the agent through whom all things were made; there is not a single thing which exists in this world which came into being without him. In him was life and the life was the light of men; and the light shines in the darkness, because the darkness has never been able to conquer it. There emerged a man sent from God whose name was John. He came as a witness, in order to bear witness to the light, that through him all might believe. He himself was not the light; his function was to bear witness to the light. He was the real light, who, in his coming into the world, gives light to every man. He was in the world, and, although the world was made by him, the world did not recognize him. It was into his own home that he came, and yet his own people did not receive him. To all those who did receive him, to those who believe in his name, he gave the right to become the children of God. These were born, not of blood, nor or any human impulse, nor of any man's will, but their birth was of God. So the word became a person, and took up his abode in our being, full of grace and truth; and we beheld his glory, glory such as an only son receives from his father. John was his witness, for he cried: "This is he of whom I said to you, he who comes after me has been advanced before me, because he was before me. On his fullness we all of us have drawn, and we have received grace upon grace, because it was the law which was given by Moses, but grace and truth came through Jesus Christ. No one has ever seen God. It is the unique one, he who is God, he who is in the bosom of the Father, who has told us all about God."

It was not long before the Christian church was confronted with a very basic problem. It had begun in Judaism. In the beginning all its members had been Jews. By human descent Jesus was a Jew, and, to all intents and purposes, except for brief visits to the districts of Tyre and Sidon, and to the Decapolis, he was never outside Palestine.

Christianity began amongst the Jews; and therefore inevitably it spoke in the Jewish language and used Jewish categories of thought.

But although it was cradled in Judaism it very soon went out into the wider world. Within thirty years of Jesus' death it had travelled all over Asia Minor and Greece and had arrived in Rome. By A.D. 60 there must have been a hundred thousand Greeks in the church for every Jew who was a Christian. Jewish ideas were completely strange to the Greeks. To take but one outstanding example, the Greeks had never heard of the Messiah. The very centre of Jewish expectation, the coming of the Messiah, was an idea that was quite alien to the Greeks. The very category in which the Jewish Christians conceived and presented Jesus meant nothing to them. Here then was the problem— how was Christianity to be presented to the Greek world?

Lecky, the historian, once said that the progress and spread of any idea depends, not only on its strength and force but on the predisposition to receive it of the age to which it is presented. The task of the Christian church was to create in the Greek world a predisposition to receive the Christian message. As E. J. Goodspeed put it, the question was, "Must a Greek who was interested in Christianity be routed through Jewish Messianic ideas and through Jewish ways of thinking, or could some new approach be found which would speak out of his background to his mind and heart?" The problem was how to present Christianity in such a way that a Greek would understand.

Round about the year A.D. 100 there was a man in Ephesus who was fascinated by that problem. His name was John. He lived in a Greek city. He dealt with Greeks to whom Jewish ideas were strange and unintelligible and even uncouth. How could he find a way to present Christianity to these Greeks in a way that they would welcome and understand? Suddenly the solution flashed upon him. In both Greek and Jewish thought there existed the conception of *the word*. Here was something which could be worked out to meet the double world of Greek and Jew. Here was something which belonged to the heritage of both races and that both could understand.

Slowly the Jews and Greeks had thought their way to the conception of the *Logos*, the Mind of God which made the world and makes sense of it. So John went out to Jews and Greeks to tell them that in Jesus Christ this creating, illuminating, controlling, sustaining Mind of God had come to earth. He came to tell them that people need no longer guess and grope; all that they had to do was to look at Jesus and see the Mind of God.

2nd Day of Lent

Luke 3:7–18

To the crowds who came out to be baptized by him, John used to say, "You spawn of vipers, who put it into your heads to flee from the coming wrath? Produce fruits to match repentance. Do not begin to say among yourselves, 'We have Abraham as our father.' I tell you that God is able to raise up children to Abraham from these stones. Even now the axe is laid at the root of the trees. Every tree that does not bear good fruit is cut down and thrown into the fire." The crowds asked him, "What are we to do?" He answered them, "Let him who has two robes give one to one who has none and let him who has food do likewise." The tax-collectors came to be baptized and said to him, "Teacher, what are we to do?" He said to them, "Exact no more beyond what your instructions lay down." The soldiers, too, asked him, "What are we to do?" He said to them, "Treat no man with violence and do not play the false informer and be content with your pay."

When the people were in a state of expectancy and when they were all wondering in their hearts about John, as to whether he could be the Anointed One, John answered them all, "I baptize you with water, but the One who is stronger than I is coming, the latchet of whose sandals I am not worthy to unloose. He will baptize you with the Holy Spirit and with fire. His winnowing fan is in his hand to cleanse his threshing floor and he will gather the corn into his store but he will burn the chaff with unquenchable fire."

Here we have the message of John to the people. Nowhere does the difference between John and Jesus stand out so clearly because, whatever the message of John was, it was not a gospel. It was not good news; it was news of terror.

John had lived in the desert. The face of the desert was covered with stubble and brushwood, as dry as tinder. Sometimes a spark set the face of the desert alight and out from their crannies came the vipers, scurrying in terror from the menacing flames. It was to them John likened the people who came to be baptized.

Luke 3:21, 22

When all the people had been baptized and when Jesus too had been baptized, as he was praying, the heaven was opened and the Holy Spirit in bodily form like a dove came down upon him and there was a voice from heaven, "You are my beloved son; in you I am well pleased."

The thinkers of the church have always sought an answer to the problem, "Why did Jesus go to John to be baptized?" The baptism of John was a baptism of repentance and it is our conviction that Jesus was without sin. Why then did he offer himself for this baptism? In the early church it was sometimes suggested, with a homely touch, that he did it to please Mary, his mother, and in answer to her entreaties; but we need a better reason than that.

In the life of every person there are certain definite stages, certain hinges on which the whole of life turns. It was so with Jesus and every now and again we must stop and try to see his life as a whole. The first great hinge was the visit to the Temple when he was twelve, when he discovered his unique relationship to God. By the time of the emergence of John, Jesus was about thirty (Luke 3:23). That is to say at least eighteen years had passed. All through these years he must have been realizing more and more his own uniqueness. But still he remained the village carpenter of Nazareth. He must have known that a day must come when he must say good-bye to Nazareth and go out upon his larger task. He must have waited for some sign.

When John emerged the people flocked out to hear him and to be baptized. Throughout the whole country there was an unprecedented movement towards God. And Jesus knew that his hour had struck. It was not that he was conscious of sin and of the need of repentance. It was that he knew that he too must identify himself with this movement towards God. For Jesus the emergence of John was God's call to action; and his first step was to identify himself with the people in their search for God.

But in Jesus' baptism something happened. Before he could take this tremendous step he had to be sure that he was right; and in the moment of baptism God spoke to him. Make no mistake, what happened in the baptism was an experience personal to Jesus. The voice of God came to him and told him that he had taken the right decision, but more—far more—that very same voice mapped out all his course for him.

God said to him, "You are my beloved Son; with you I am well pleased." That saying is composed of two texts. *You are my beloved Son*—that is from Psalm 2:7 and was always accepted as a description of the Messianic King. *In whom I am well pleased*—that is part of Isaiah 42:1 and is from a description of the servant of the Lord whose portrait culminates in the sufferings of Isaiah 53. Therefore in his baptism Jesus realized, first, that he was the Messiah, God's Anointed King; and, second, that this involved not power and glory, but suffering and a cross. The cross did not come on Jesus unawares; from the first moment of realization he saw it ahead. The baptism shows us Jesus asking for God's approval and receiving the destiny of the cross.

3rd Day of Lent

Mark 1:12, 13
And immediately the Spirit thrust him into the wilderness. He was in the wilderness forty days, and all the time he was being tested by Satan. The wild beasts were his companions, and the angels were helping him.

No sooner was the glory of the hour of the baptism over than there came the battle of the temptations. One thing stands out here in such a vivid way that we cannot miss it. It was the Spirit who thrust Jesus out into the wilderness for the testing time. The very Spirit who came upon him at his baptism now drove him out for his test.

In this life it is impossible to escape the assault of temptation; but one thing is sure—temptations are not sent to us to make us fall; they are sent to strengthen the nerve and the sinew of our minds and hearts and souls. They are not meant for our ruin, but for our good. They are meant to be tests from which we emerge better warriors and athletes of God.

"Forty days" is a phrase which is not to be taken literally. It is the regular Hebrew phrase for a considerable time. Moses was said to be on the mountain with God for "forty days" (Exodus 24:18); it was for "forty days" that Elijah went in the strength of the meal the angel gave him (1 Kings 19:8). Just as we use the phrase "ten days or so," so the Hebrews used the phrase "forty days," not literally but simply to mean a fair length of time.

It was Satan who tempted Jesus. The development of the conception of Satan is very interesting. The word "Satan" in Hebrew simply means "an *adversary*"; and in the Old Testament it is so used of ordinary human adversaries and opponents again and again. The angel of the Lord is the *satan* who stands in Balaam's way (Numbers 22:22); the Philistines fear that David may turn out to be their *satan* (1 Samuel 29:4); David regards Abishai as his *satan* (2 Samuel 19:22); Solomon declares that God has given him such peace and prosperity that he has no *satan* left to oppose him (1 Kings 5:4). The word began by meaning "an adversary" in the widest sense of the term. But it takes a step on the downward path; it begins to mean one who pleads a case against a person. It is in this sense that it is used in the first chapter of Job. In that chapter Satan is no less than one of the sons of God (Job 1:6); but his particular task was to consider humankind (Job 1:7) and to search for some case that could be pleaded against them in the presence of God. He was the accuser of people before God. The word is so used in Job 2:2 and Zechariah 3:2. The task of Satan was to say everything that could be said against a person.

The other title of Satan is the *Devil;* the word *devil* comes from the Greek *diabolos,* which literally means "a slanderer." It is a small step from the thought of one who searches for everything that can be said against a person to the thought of one who deliberately and maliciously slanders people in the presence of God. But in the Old Testament Satan is still an emissary of God and not yet the malignant, supreme enemy of God. He is the "adversary of humanity."

When we turn to the New Testament we find that it is the Devil or Satan who is behind human disease and suffering (Luke 13:16); it is Satan who seduces Judas (Luke 22:3); it is the devil whom we must fight (1 Peter 5:8, 9; James 4:7); it is the devil whose power is being broken by the work of Christ (Luke 10:1–19); it is the devil who is destined for final destruction (Matthew 25:41). Satan is the power which is against God.

Here we have the whole essence of the Temptation story. Jesus had to decide how he was to do his work. He was conscious of a tremendous task and he was also conscious of tremendous powers. God was saying to him, "Take my love to all people; love them till you die for them; conquer them by this unconquerable love even if you finish up upon a cross." Satan was saying to Jesus, "Use your power to blast people; obliterate your enemies; win the world by might and power and bloodshed." God said to Jesus, "Set up a reign of love." Satan said to Jesus, "Set up a dictatorship of force." Jesus had to choose that day between the way of God and the way of the Adversary of God.

"*The angels were helping him.*" There are ever the divine reinforcements in the hour of trial. When Elisha and his servant were shut up in Dothan with their enemies pressing in upon them and no apparent way of escape, Elisha opened the young man's eyes and all around he saw the horses and the chariots of fire which belonged to God (2 Kings 6:17). Jesus was not left to fight his battle alone—and neither are we.

4th Day of Lent

Mark 8:27–30

Jesus and his disciples went away to the villages of Caesarea Philippi. On the road he asked his disciples a question. "Who," he said to them, "do men say that I am?" They said to him, "Some say, John the Baptizer; others say, Elijah; others, one of the prophets." He asked them, "You—who do you say that I am?" Peter answered him, "You are God's Anointed One." And he insisted that they should tell no man about him.

Caesarea Philippi was outside Galilee altogether. It was not in the territory of Herod, but in the territory of Philip. It was a town with an amazing history. In the oldest days it was called *Balinas*, for it had once been a great centre of the worship of Baal. To this day it is called *Banias*, which is a form of *Panias*. It is so called because up on the hillside there was a cavern which was said to be the birthplace of the Greek God, Pan, the god of nature. From a cave in the hillside gushed forth a stream which was held to be the source of the River Jordan. Farther up on the hillside rose a gleaming temple of white marble which Philip had built to the godhead of Caesar, the Roman Emperor, the ruler of the world, who was regarded as a god.

It is an amazing thing that it was here of all places that Peter saw in a homeless Galilaean carpenter the Son of God. The ancient religion of Palestine was in the air, and the memories of Baal clustered around. The gods of classical Greece brooded over the place, and no doubt passersby heard the pipes of Pan and caught a glimpse of the woodland nymphs. The Jordan would bring back to memory episode after episode in the history of Israel and the conquest of the land. And clear in the eastern sun gleamed and glinted the marble of the holy place which reminded all men that Caesar was a god. There, of all places, as it were against the background of all religions and all history, Peter discovered that a wandering teacher from Nazareth, who was heading for a cross, was the Son of God. There is hardly anything in all the Gospel story which shows the sheer force of the personality of Jesus as does this incident. It comes in the very middle of Mark's Gospel and it does so designedly, for it comes at the Gospel's peak moment. In one way at least this moment was the crisis of Jesus' life. Whatever his disciples might be thinking, he knew for certain that ahead lay an inescapable cross. Things could not go on much longer. The opposition was gathering itself to strike. The problem confronting Jesus was this—had he had any effect at all? Had he achieved anything? Or, to put it another way, had anyone discovered who he really was? If he had lived and taught and moved amongst men and no one had glimpsed God in him, then all his work had gone for nothing. There was only one way he could leave a message with people and that was to write it on someone's heart.

So, in this moment, Jesus put all things to the test. He asked his disciples what men were saying about him, and he heard from them the popular rumours and reports. Then came a breathless silence and he put the question which meant so much, "Who do you say that I am?" And suddenly Peter realized what he had always known deep down in his heart. This was the Messiah, the Christ, the Anointed One, the Son of God. And with that answer Jesus knew that he had not failed.

Throughout all their existence the Jews never forgot that they were in a very special sense God's chosen people. Because of that, they naturally looked to a very special place in the world. In the early days they looked forward to achieving that position by what we might call natural means. They always regarded the greatest days in their history as the days of David; and they dreamed of a day when there would arise another king of David's line, a king who would make them great in righteousness and in power (Isaiah 9:7; 11:1; Jeremiah 22:4; 23:5; 30:9).

But as time went on it came to be pitilessly clear that this dreamed-of greatness would never be achieved by natural means. The ten tribes were carried off to Assyria and lost forever. The Babylonians conquered Jerusalem and carried the Jews away captive. Then came the Persians as their masters; then the Greeks; then the Romans. So far from knowing anything like dominion, for centuries the Jews never even knew what it was to be completely free and independent. So another line of thought grew up. It is true that the idea of a great king of David's line never entirely vanished and was always intertwined in some way with their thought; but more and more they began to dream of a day when God would intervene in history and achieve by supernatural means that which natural means could never achieve. They looked for divine power to do what human power was helpless to do.

First Sunday in Lent

Mark 9:2–8

Six days after, Jesus took Peter and James and John along with him and brought them up into a high mountain, all by themselves, alone. And he was transfigured in their presence. His clothes became radiant, exceedingly white, such that no fuller on earth could have made them so white.

And Elijah and Moses appeared to them, and they were talking with Jesus. Peter said to Jesus, "Teacher, it is good for us to be here. So let us make three booths, one for you, and one for Moses and one for Elijah." He said this because he did not know what he was saying, for they were awestruck. And there came a cloud overshadowing them. And there came a voice from the cloud, "This is my beloved Son. Hear Him!" And immediately, when they had looked round, they saw no one any more except Jesus alone with them.

We are face to face with an incident in the life of Jesus that is cloaked in mystery. We can only try to understand. Mark says that this happened six days after the incidents near Caesarea Philippi. Luke says that it happened eight days afterwards. There is no discrepancy here. They both mean what we might express by saying, "About a week afterwards." Both the Eastern and the Western Churches hold their remembrance of the transfiguration on 6th August. It does not matter whether or not that is the actual date, but it is a time we do well to remember.

Tradition says that the transfiguration took place on the top of Mount Tabor. The Eastern Church actually calls the Festival of the Transfiguration the "Taborion." It may be that the choice is based on the mention of Mount Tabor in Psalm 89:12, but it is unfortunate. Tabor is in the south of Galilee and Caesarea Philippi is away to the north. Tabor is no more than 1,000 feet high, and, in the time of Jesus, there was a fortress on the top. It is much more likely that this event took place amidst the eternal snows of Mount Hermon which is 9,200 feet high and much nearer Caesarea Philippi and where the solitude would be much more complete.

What happened we cannot tell. We can only bow in reverence as we try to understand. Mark tells us that the garments of Jesus became radiant. The word he uses (*stilbein*) is the word used for the glistening gleam of burnished brass or gold or of polished steel or of the golden glare of the sunlight. When the incident came to an end a cloud overshadowed them.

In Jewish thought the presence of God is regularly connected with the cloud. It was in the cloud that Moses met God. It was in the cloud that God came to the Tabernacle. It was the cloud which filled the Temple when it was dedicated after Solomon had built it. And it was the dream of the Jews that when the Messiah came the cloud of God's presence would return to the Temple (Exodus 16:10; 19:9; 33:9; 1 Kings 8:10; 2 Maccabees 2:8). The descent of the cloud is a way of saying that the Messiah had come, and any Jew would understand it like that.

The transfiguration has a double significance.

(i) It did something very precious for Jesus. Jesus had to take his own decisions. He had taken the decision to go to Jerusalem and that was the decision to face and accept the Cross. Obviously he had to be absolutely sure that was right before he could go on. On the mountaintop he received a double approval of his decision.

(a) Moses and Elijah met with him. Now Moses was the supreme law-giver of Israel. To him the nation owed the laws of God. Elijah was the first and the greatest of the prophets. Always men looked back to him as the prophet who brought to men the very voice of God. When these two great figures met with Jesus it meant that the greatest of the law-givers and the greatest of the prophets said to him, "Go on!" It meant that they saw in Jesus the consummation of all that they had dreamed of in the past. It meant that they saw in him all that history had longed for and hoped for and looked forward to. It is as if at that moment Jesus was assured that he was on the right way because all history had been leading up to the Cross.

(b) God spoke with Jesus. As always, Jesus did not consult his own wishes. He went to God and said, "What wilt thou have me to do?" He put all his plans and intentions before God. And God said to him, "You are acting as my own beloved Son should act and must act. Go on!" On the mountain of the transfiguration Jesus was assured that he had not chosen the wrong way. He saw, not only the inevitability, but the essential rightness of the cross.

(ii) It did something very precious for the disciples.

(a) They had been shattered by Jesus' statement that he was going to Jerusalem to die. That seemed to them the complete negation of all that they understood of the Messiah. They were still bewildered and uncomprehending. Things were happening which not only baffled their minds but were also breaking their hearts. What they saw on the mountain of the transfiguration would give them something to hold on to, even when they could not understand. Cross or no cross, they had heard God's voice acknowledge Jesus as his Son.

(b) It made them in a special sense witnesses of the glory of Christ. A witness has been defined as a man who first sees and then shows. This time on the mountain had shown them the glory of Christ, and now they had the story of this glory to hide in their hearts and to tell to men, not at the moment, but when the time came.

5th Day of Lent

Mark 8:22–26

They came to Bethsaida; and they brought a blind man to him and asked him to touch him. He took the blind man's hand and took him outside the village. He spat into his eyes and laid his hands on him, and asked him, "Do you see anything?" He looked up and said, "I see men, but I see them walking looking like trees." Again he laid his hands on his eyes. He gazed intently, and his sight was restored and he saw everything clearly. He sent him away to his home. "Do not," he said, "even enter into the village."

Blindness was, and still is, one of the great curses of the East. It was caused partly by ophthalmia and partly by the pitiless glare of the sun. It was greatly aggravated by the fact that people knew nothing of hygiene and of cleanliness. It was common to see a person with matter-encrusted eyes on which the flies persistently settled. Naturally this carried the infection far and wide, and blindness was a scourge.

Only Mark tells us this story, and yet there are certain extremely interesting things in it.

(i) Again we see the unique considerateness of Jesus. He took the blind man out of the crowd and out of the village that he might be alone with him. Why? Think about it. This man was blind and apparently had been born blind. If he had been suddenly given back his sight amidst a crowd, there would have flashed upon his newly-seeing eyes hundreds of people and things, and dazzling colours, so that he would have been completely bewildered. Jesus knew it would be far better if he could be taken to a place where the thrill of seeing would break less suddenly upon him.

(ii) Jesus used methods that the man could understand. The ancient world believed in the healing power of spittle. The belief is not so strange when we remember that it is a first instinct to put a cut or burned finger into our mouth to ease the pain. Of course the blind man knew of this and Jesus used a method of curing him which he could understand. Jesus was wise. He did not begin with words and methods which were far above the heads of simple folk. He spoke to them and acted on them in a way that simple minds could grasp and understand. There have been times when unintelligibility has been accounted a virtue and a sign of greatness. Jesus had the still greater greatness—the greatness which a simple mind could grasp.

(iii) In one thing this miracle is unique—it is the only miracle which can be said to have happened gradually. Usually Jesus' miracles happened suddenly and completely. In this miracle the blind man's sight came back in stages.

There is symbolic truth here. No one sees all God's truth all at once. One of the dangers of a certain type of evangelism is that it encourages the idea that when people have taken a decision for Christ they are full-grown Christians. One of the dangers of church membership is that it can be presented in such a way as to imply that when we become pledged members of the church we have come to the end of the road. So far from that being the case. The decision and the pledge of membership are the beginning of the road; they are the discovery of the riches of Christ which are inexhaustible, and if we lived a hundred, or a thousand, or a million years, we would still have to go on growing in grace, and learning more and more about the infinite wonder and beauty of Jesus Christ. F. W. H. Myers, in his poem "Saint Paul" makes Paul say:

Let no man think that sudden in a minute
All is accomplished and the work is done—
Though with thine earliest dawn thou shouldst begin it
Scarce were it ended in thy setting sun.

It is gloriously true that sudden conversion is a gracious possibility, but it is equally true that every day we should be re-converted. With all God's grace and glory before us, we can go on learning for a life time and still need eternity to know as we are known.

6th Day of Lent

Mark 8:11–13

The Pharisees came out and began to ask him questions. They were looking for a sign from heaven, and they were trying to test him. He sighed in his spirit and said to them, "Why does this generation look for a sign? This is the truth I tell you—no sign will be given to this generation." He sent them away and he again embarked on the boat, and went away to the other side.

The whole tendency of the age in which Jesus lived was to look for God in the abnormal. It was believed that when the Messiah came the most startling things would happen. Before we reach the end of this chapter we shall examine more closely, and in detail, the kind of signs which were expected. We may note just now that when false Messiahs arose, as they frequently did, they lured the people to follow them by promising astonishing signs. They would promise, for instance, to cleave the waters of the Jordan in two and leave a pathway through it, or they would promise, with a word, to make the city walls fall down.

It was a sign like that that the Pharisees were demanding. They wished to see some shattering event blazing across the horizon, defying the laws of nature and astonishing mortals. To Jesus such a demand was not due to the desire to see the hand of God; it was due to the fact that they were blind to his hand. To Jesus the whole world was full of signs; the corn in the field, the leaven in the loaf, the scarlet anemones on the hillside all spoke to him of God. He did not think that God had to break in from outside the world; he knew that God was already in the world for anyone who had eyes to see. The sign of truly religious persons is not that they come to Church to find God but that they find God everywhere, not that they make a great deal of sacred places but that they sanctify common places.

That is what the poets knew and felt, and that is why they were poets. Elizabeth Barrett Browning wrote:

Earth's crammed with heaven,
And every common bush afire with God;
But only he who sees, takes off his shoes,
The rest sit round it and pluck blackberries.

For those who have eyes to see and hearts to understand, the daily miracle of night and day and the daily splendour of all common things are signs enough from God.

7th Day of Lent

John 4:1–9

So when the Lord learned that the Pharisees had heard that Jesus was making and baptizing more disciples than John (although it was not Jesus himself who was in the habit of baptizing but his disciples), he quitted Judaea and went away again to Galilee. Now he had to pass through Samaria. He came to a town of Samaria, called Sychar, which is near the piece of ground which Jacob gave to Joseph, his son, and Jacob's well was there. So Jesus, tired from the journey, was sitting by the well just as he was. It was about midday. There came a woman of Samaria to draw water. Jesus said to her: "Give me to drink." For his disciples had gone away into the town to buy provisions. So the Samaritan woman said to him: "How is it that you who are a Jew ask a drink from me, a Samaritan woman?" (For there is no familiarity between Jews and Samaritans.)

When Jesus and his little band came to the fork in the road Jesus sat down to rest, for he was tired with the journey. It was midday. The Jewish day runs from 6 A.M. to 6 P.M. and the sixth hour is twelve o'clock midday. So the heat was at its greatest, and Jesus was weary and thirsty from travelling. His disciples went on ahead to buy some food in the Samaritan town. Something must have been beginning to happen to them. Before they had met Jesus it is entirely unlikely that they would have even thought of buying food in any Samaritan town. Little by little, perhaps even unconsciously, the barriers were going down.

Few stories in the Gospel record show us so much about the character of Jesus.

(i) It shows us the reality of his humanity. Jesus was weary with the journey, and he sat by the side of the well exhausted. It is very significant that John who stresses the sheer deity of Jesus Christ more than any other of the Gospel writers also stresses his humanity to the full. John does not show us a figure freed from the tiredness and the struggle of our humanity. He shows us one for whom life was an effort as it is for us; he shows us one who also was tired and had to go on.

(ii) It shows us the warmth of his sympathy. From an ordinary religious leader, from one of the orthodox church leaders of the day the Samaritan woman would have fled in embarrassment. She would have avoided such a one. If by any unlikely chance he had spoken to her she would have met him with an ashamed and even a hostile silence. But it seemed the most natural thing in the world to talk to Jesus. She had at last met someone who was not a critic but a friend, one who did not condemn but who understood.

(iii) It shows us Jesus as the breaker down of barriers. The quarrel between the Jews and the Samaritans was an old, old story. Away back about 720 B.C. the Assyrians had invaded the northern kingdom of Samaria and had captured and subjugated it. They did what conquerors often did in those days—they transported practically the whole population to Media (2 Kings 17:6). Into the district the Assyrians brought other people—from Babylon, from Cuthah, from Ava, from Hamath and from Sepharvaim (2 Kings 17:24). Now it is not possible to transport a whole people. Some of the people of the northern kingdom were left. Almost inevitably they began to inter-marry with the incoming foreigners; and thereby they committed what to the Jew was an unforgivable crime. They lost their racial purity.

The Jewish-Samaritan quarrel was more than 400 years old. But it smouldered as resentfully and as bitterly as ever. It was small wonder that the Samaritan woman was astonished that Jesus, a Jew, should speak to her, a Samaritan.

(iv) But there was still another way in which Jesus was taking down the barriers. The Samaritan was a woman. The strict rabbis forbade a rabbi to greet a woman in public. A rabbi might not even speak to his own wife or daughter or sister in public. There were even Pharisees who were called "the bruised and bleeding Pharisees" because they shut their eyes when they saw a woman on the street and so walked into walls and houses! For a rabbi to be seen speaking to a woman in public was the end of his reputation—and yet Jesus spoke to this woman. Not only was she a woman; she was also a woman of notorious character. No decent man, let alone a rabbi, would have been seen in her company, or even exchanging a word with her—and yet Jesus spoke to her.

To a Jew this was an amazing story. Here was the Son of God, tired and weary and thirsty. Here was the holiest of men, listening with understanding to a sorry story. Here was Jesus breaking through the barriers of nationality and orthodox Jewish custom. Here is the beginning of the universality of the gospel; here is God so loving the world, not in theory, but in action.

8th Day of Lent

Luke 11:5–13

Jesus said to them, "Suppose one of you has a friend and goes to him towards midnight and says to him, 'Friend, lend me three loaves because a friend of mine has arrived at my house from a journey and I have nothing to set before him'; and suppose his friend answers from within, 'Don't bother me; the door has already been shut and my children are in bed with me; I can't get up and supply you'—I tell you, if he will not rise and supply him because he is his friend, he will rise and give him as much as he needs because of his shameless persistence. For I say to you, 'Ask and it will be given to you; seek and you will find; knock and it will be opened to you. For everyone who asks receives; and he who seeks finds; and to him who knocks it will be opened. If a son asks any father among you for bread, will he give him a stone? Or, if he asks a fish, will he, instead of a fish, give him a serpent? Or if he asks an egg, will he give him a scorpion? If you then, who are evil, know to give good gifts to your children, how much more will your Father who is in Heaven give the Holy Spirit to those who ask him?' "

Travellers often journeyed late in the evening to avoid the heat of the midday sun. In Jesus' story just such a traveller had arrived towards midnight at this friend's house. In the east hospitality is a sacred duty; it was not enough to set before a visitor a bare sufficiency; the guest had to be confronted with an ample abundance. In the villages bread was baked at home. Only enough for the day's needs was baked because, if it was kept and became stale, no one would wish to eat it.

The late arrival of the traveller confronted the householder with an embarrassing situation, because his larder was empty and he could not fulfil the sacred obligations of hospitality. Late as it was, he went out to borrow from a friend. The friend's door was shut. In the east no one would knock on a shut door unless the need was imperative. In the morning the door was opened and remained open all day, for there was little privacy; but if the door was shut, that was a definite sign that the householder did not wish to be disturbed. But the seeking householder was not deterred. He knocked, and kept on knocking.

The poorer Palestinian house consisted of one room with only one little window. The floor was simply of beaten earth covered with dried reeds and rushes. The room was divided into two parts, not by a partition but by a low platform. Two-thirds of it were on ground level. The other third was slightly raised. On the raised part the charcoal stove burned all night, and round it the whole family slept, not on raised beds but on sleeping mats. Families were large and they slept close together for warmth. For one to rise was inevitably to disturb the whole family. Further, in the villages it was the custom to bring the livestock, the hens and the cocks and the goats, into the house at night.

Is there any wonder that the man who was in bed did not want to rise? But the determined borrower knocked on with shameless persistence—that is what the Greek word means—until at last the householder, knowing that by this time the whole family was disturbed anyway, arose and gave him what he needed.

"That story," said Jesus, "will tell you about prayer." The lesson of this parable is not that we must persist in prayer; it is not that we must batter at God's door until we finally compel him for very weariness to give us what we want, until we coerce an unwilling God to answer.

A parable literally means "something laid alongside." If we lay something beside another thing to teach a lesson, that lesson may be drawn from the fact that the things are like each other or from the fact that the things are a contrast to each other. The point here is based, not on likeness, but on contrast. What Jesus says is, "If a churlish and unwilling householder can in the end be coerced by a friend's shameless persistence into giving him what he needs, how much more will God who is a loving Father supply all his children's needs?" "If you," he says, "who are evil, know that you are bound to supply your children's needs, how much more will God?"

This does not absolve us from intensity in prayer. After all, we can guarantee the reality and sincerity of our desire only by the passion with which we pray. But it does mean this, that we are not wringing gifts from an unwilling God, but going to one who knows our needs better than we know them ourselves and whose heart towards us is the heart of generous love. If we do not receive what we pray for, it is not because God grudgingly refuses to give it but because he has some better thing for us. There is no such thing as unanswered prayer. The answer given may not be the answer we desired or expected; but even when it is a refusal it is the answer of the love and the wisdom of God.

9th Day of Lent

Matthew 16:24–26

Then Jesus said to his disciples: "If anyone wishes to come after me, let him deny himself, and take up his cross, and let him follow me. For whoever wishes to keep his life safe, will lose it; and whoever loses his life for my sake, will find it. For what shall a man be profited if he shall gain the whole world at the penalty of the price of his life? Or what will a man give in exchange for his life?"

Here we have one of the dominant and ever-recurring themes of Jesus' teaching. These are things which Jesus said again and again (Matthew 10:37–39; Mark 8:34–37; Luke 9:23–27; 14:25–27; 17:33; John 12:25). Again and again he presented with the challenge of the Christian life. There are three things which one must be prepared to do, if one is to live the Christian life.

(i) Jesus' followers must deny themselves. Ordinarily we use the word self-denial in a restricted sense. We use it to mean giving up something. For instance, a week of self-denial may be a week when we do without certain pleasures or luxuries in order to contribute to some good cause. But that is only a very small part of what Jesus meant by self-denial. To deny oneself means in every moment of life to say no to self and yes to God. To deny oneself means once, finally and for all to dethrone self and to enthrone God. To deny oneself means to obliterate self as the dominant principle of life, and to make God the ruling principle, more, the ruling passion, of life. The life of constant self-denial is the life of constant assent to God.

(ii) Disciples must take up each their own cross. That is to say, each one must take up the burden of sacrifice. The Christian life is the life of sacrificial service. Christians may have to abandon personal ambition to serve Christ; it may be that they will discover that the place where they can render the greatest service to Jesus Christ is somewhere where the reward will be small and the prestige non-existent. They will certainly have to sacrifice time and leisure and pleasure in order to serve God through the service of those around them.

Luke, with a flash of sheer insight, adds one word to this command of Jesus: Disciples are to take up the cross "daily." The really important thing is not the great moments of sacrifice, but a life lived in the constant hourly awareness of the demands of God and the need of others. The Christian life is a life which is always concerned with others more than it is concerned with itself.

(iii) Each must follow Jesus Christ. That is to say, each must render to Jesus Christ a perfect obedience. When we were young we used to play a game called "Follow my Leader." Everything the leader did, however difficult, and, in the case of the game, however ridiculous, we had to copy. The Christian life is a constant following of our leader, a constant obedience in thought and word and action to Jesus Christ. The Christian walks in the footsteps of Christ, wherever they may lead.

In our day and generation it is not likely to be a question of martyrdom, but it still remains a fact that, if we meet life in the constant search for safety, security, ease and comfort, if every decision is taken from worldly-wise and prudential motives, we are losing all that makes life worthwhile. Life becomes a soft and flabby thing, when it might have been an adventure. Life becomes a selfish thing, when it might have been radiant with service. Life becomes an earthbound thing when it might have been reaching for the stars. Someone once wrote a bitter epitaph on a man: "He was born a man and died a grocer." Any trade or profession might be substituted for the word grocer. The one who plays for safety ceases to be a human being, for humans are made in the image of God.

(iv) Those who risk all—and maybe look as if they had lost all—for Christ find life. It is the simple lesson of history that it has always been the adventurous souls, bidding farewell to security and safety, who wrote their names on history and greatly helped the world. Unless there had been those prepared to take risks, many a medical cure would not exist. Unless there had been those prepared to take risks, many of the machines which make life easier would never have been invented. Unless there were mothers prepared to take risks, no child would ever be born. It is those who are prepared to bet life itself that there is a God, who in the end find life.

10th Day of Lent

Mark 10:35–40

James and John, the sons of Zebedee, came to Jesus. "Teacher," they said, "we want you to do for us whatever we ask you." "What do you want me to do for you?" he said to them. They said to him, "Grant to us that, in your glory, we may sit one on your right hand and one on your left." "You do not know what you ask," Jesus said to them. "Can you drink the cup which I am drinking? Or, can you go through the experience through which I am going?" "We can," they said to him. Jesus said to them, "You will drink the cup which I am drinking. You will go through the experience through which I am going. But to sit on my right hand and on my left is not mine to give you. That place belongs to those for whom it has been prepared."

This is a very revealing story.

(i) It tells us something about Mark. Matthew retells this story (Matthew 20:20–23), but in his version the request for the first places is made not by James and John, but by their mother Salome. Matthew must have felt that such a request was unworthy of an apostle, and, to save the reputation of James and John, he attributed it to the natural ambition of their mother. This story shows us the honesty of Mark.

(ii) It tells us something about James and John.

(a) It tells us that they were ambitious. When the victory was won and the triumph was complete, they aimed at being Jesus' chief ministers of state. Maybe their ambition was kindled because more than once Jesus had made them part of his inner circle, the chosen three. Maybe they were a little better off than the others. Their father was well enough off to employ hired servants (Mark 1:20), and it may be that they rather snobbishly thought that their social superiority entitled them to the first place. In any event they show themselves as persons in whose hearts there was ambition for the first place in an earthly kingdom.

(b) It tells us that they had completely failed to understand Jesus. The amazing thing is not the fact that this incident happened, but the time at which it happened. It is the juxtaposition of Jesus' most definite and detailed forecast of his death and this request that is staggering. It shows, as nothing else could, how little they understood what Jesus was saying to them. Words were powerless to rid them of the idea of a Messiah of earthly power and glory. Only the cross could do that.

(c) But when we have said all that is to be said against James and John, this story tells us one shining thing about them—bewildered as they might be, they still believed in Jesus. It is amazing that they could still connect glory with a Galilaean carpenter who had incurred the enmity and the bitter opposition of the orthodox religious leaders and who was apparently heading for a cross. There is amazing confidence and amazing loyalty there. Misguided James and John might be but their hearts were in the right place. They never doubted Jesus' ultimate triumph.

(iii) It tells us something of Jesus' standard of greatness. The Revised Standard Version gives a literally accurate reading of what Jesus said—"Are you able to drink the cup that I drink, or to be baptized with the baptism with which I am baptized?" Jesus uses two Jewish metaphors here.

It was the custom at a royal banquet for the king to hand the cup to his guests. "The cup" therefore became a metaphor for the life and experience that God handed out to humans. "My cup overflows," said the Psalmist (Psalm 23:5), when he spoke of a life and experience of happiness given to him by God. "In the hand of the Lord there is a cup," said the Psalmist (Psalm 75:8), when he was thinking of the fate in store for the wicked and the disobedient. Isaiah, thinking of the disasters which had come upon the people of Israel, describes them as having drunk "at the hand of the Lord the cup of his wrath." (Isaiah 51:17.) The cup speaks of the experience allotted to people by God.

The other phrase which Jesus uses is actually misleading in the literal English version. He speaks of the baptism with which he was baptized. The Greek verb *baptizein* means "to dip." Its past participle (*bebaptismenos*) means "submerged," and it is regularly used for being submerged in any experience. For instance, a spendthrift is said to be submerged in debt. A drunk is said to be submerged in drink. A grief-stricken person is said to be submerged in sorrow. A pupil before a cross-examining teacher is said to be submerged in questions. The word is regularly used for a ship that has been wrecked and submerged beneath the waves. The metaphor is very closely related to a metaphor which the Psalmist often uses. In Psalm 42:7 we read, "All thy waves and thy billows have gone over me." In Psalm 124:4 we read, "Then the flood would have swept us away, the torrent would have gone over us." The expression, as Jesus used it here, had nothing to do with technical baptism. What he is saying is, "Can you bear to go through the terrible experience which I have to go through? Can you face being submerged in hatred and pain and death, as I have to be?" He was telling these two disciples that without a cross there can never be a crown. The standard of greatness in the Kingdom is the standard of the cross. It was true that in the days to come they did go through the experience of their Master, for James was beheaded by Herod Agrippa (Acts 12:2), and, though John was probably not martyred, he suffered much for Christ. They accepted the challenge of their Master—even if they did so blindly.

(iv) Jesus told them that the ultimate issue of things belonged to God. The final assignment of destiny was his prerogative. Jesus never usurped the place of God. His own whole life was one long act of submission to his will and he knew that in the end that will was supreme.

Second Sunday in Lent

Mark 10:41–45

When the ten heard about this, they began to be vexed about the action of James and John. Jesus called them to him. "You are well aware," he said, "that those who are esteemed good enough to rule over the Gentiles lord it over them, and their great ones exercise authority over them. It is not so amongst you, but, amongst you, whoever wishes to be great will be your servant, and amongst you, whoever wishes to be first will be the slave of all. For the Son of Man did not come to be served but to serve, and to give his life a ransom for many."

This was a serious situation. The fellowship of the apostolic band might well have been wrecked, had Jesus not taken immediate action. He called them to him, and made quite clear the different standards of greatness in his Kingdom and in the kingdoms of the world. In the kingdoms of the world the standard of greatness was power. The test was: How many people does a person control? How great an army of servants are at beck and call? On how many others can one impose one's will? In the Kingdom of Jesus the standard was that of service. Greatness consisted, not in reducing others to one's service, but in reducing oneself to their service. The test was not, What service can I extract? but, What service can I give?

To clinch his words Jesus pointed to his own example. With such powers as he had, he could have arranged life entirely to suit himself, but he had spent himself and all his powers in the service of others. He had come, he said, "*to give his life a ransom for many.*" This is one of the great phrases of the gospel, and yet it has been sadly mishandled and maltreated. People have tried to erect a theory of the atonement on what is a saying of love.

It was not long until people were asking to whom this ransom of the life of Christ had been paid. Origen asked the question, "To whom did he give his life a ransom for many? It was not to God. Was it not then to the Evil One? For the devil was holding us fast until the ransom should be given to him, even the life of Jesus, for he was deceived with the idea that he could have dominion over it and did not see that he could not bear the torture involved in retaining it." It is an odd conception that the life of Jesus was paid as a ransom to the devil so that he should release humans from the bondage in which he held them, but that the devil found that in demanding and accepting that ransom, he had, so to speak, bitten off more than he could chew.

Gregory of Nyssa saw the flaw in that theory, namely that it really puts the devil on an equality with God. It allows him to make a bargain with God on equal terms. So Gregory of Nyssa conceived of the extraordinary idea of a trick played by God. The devil was tricked by the seeming weakness of the incarnation. He mistook Jesus for a mere mortal. He tried to exert his authority over him and, by trying to do so, lost it. Again it is an odd idea—that God should conquer the devil by a trick.

Another two hundred years passed and Gregory the Great took up the idea. He used a fantastic metaphor. The incarnation was a divine stratagem to catch the great leviathan. The deity of Christ was the hook, his flesh was the bait. When the bait was dangled before

Leviathan, the devil, he swallowed it, and tried to swallow the hook, too, and so was overcome forever.

Finally Peter the Lombard brings this idea to its most grotesque and repulsive. "The Cross," he said, "was a mouse-trap to catch the devil, baited with the blood of Christ." All this simply shows what happens when people take a lovely and precious picture and try to make a cold theology out of it.

Suppose we say, "Sorrow is the price of love." We mean that love cannot exist without the possibility of sorrow, but we never even think of trying to explain to whom that price is paid. Suppose we say that freedom can be obtained only at the price of blood, toil, tears and sweat, we never think of investigating to whom that price is paid. This saying of Jesus is a simple and pictorial way of saying that it cost the life of Jesus to bring humans back from their sin into the love of God. It means that the cost of our salvation was the cross of Christ. Beyond that we cannot go, and beyond that we do not need to go. We know only that something happened on the cross which opened for us the way to God.

11th Day of Lent

Mark 12:18–27

There came to Jesus Sadducees, who are a party who say that the resurrection of the dead does not exist. They put the following problem to him. "Teacher," they said, "Moses wrote the law for us, that, if a man's brother dies and leaves behind him a wife, and does not leave a family, the law is that the brother should take his wife, and should raise up a family to his brother. There were seven brothers. The first took a wife, and died, and left no family. The second took her, and he died, and left behind no family. The third did the same. The seven left no family. Last of all, the woman died. At the resurrection whose wife will she be? For the seven had her as wife." Jesus said to them, "Are you not in error and for this reason—because you do not know the scriptures, nor do you know the power of God? When people rise from the dead, they neither marry, nor are they given in marriage, but they are like the angels in heaven. With regard to the dead, and the fact that they do rise, have you not read in the Book of

Moses, in the passage about the bush, how God said to him, 'I am the God of Abraham, and the God of Isaac, and the God of Jacob.' God is not the God of the dead, but the God of the living. You are far wrong."

This is the only time in Mark's Gospel that the Sadducees appear, and their appearance is entirely characteristic of them. The Sadducees were not a large Jewish party. They were aristocratic and wealthy. They included most of the priests; the office of high priest was regularly held by a Sadducee. Being the wealthy and aristocratic party, they were not unnaturally collaborationist, for they wished to retain their comforts and their privileges. It was from them came those who were prepared to collaborate with the Romans in the government of the country.

They differed very widely from the Pharisees in certain matters. First, they accepted only the written scriptures and attached more importance to the Pentateuch, the first five books of the Old Testament, than to all the rest. They did not accept the mass of oral law and tradition, the rules and regulations which were so dear to the Pharisees. It was on the written Mosaic Law that they took their stand. Second, they did not believe in immortality, nor in spirits and angels. They said that in the early books of the Bible there was no evidence for immortality, and they did not accept it.

So the Sadducees came to Jesus with a test question designed to make the belief in individual resurrection look ridiculous. The Jewish Law had an institution called levirate marriage. Its regulations are laid down in Deuteronomy 25:5–10. If a group of brothers lived together—that is a point that is omitted in the Sadducees' quotation of the law—and if one of them died and left no issue, it was the duty of the next to take his brother's widow as wife and to raise up issue to his brother. Theoretically this would go on so long as there were brothers left and so long as no child was born. When a child was born, the child was held to be the offspring of the original husband.

It is clear that the whole point of this law was to ensure two things—first, that the family name continued, and second, that the property remained within the family.

The question that the Sadducees asked, therefore, may have presented an exaggerated case, with the story of the seven brothers, but it was a question founded on a well-known Jewish law. The question of the Sadducees was simply this—if, in accordance with the regulations governing levirate marriage, one woman has been married in turn to seven brothers, if there is a resurrection of the dead, whose wife is she when that resurrection comes? They thought that by asking that question they rendered the idea of resurrection completely ridiculous. Jesus' answer really falls into two parts.

First, he deals with what we might call the manner of the resurrection. He lays it down that when a person rises again, the old laws of physical life no longer obtain. The risen are like the angels, and physical things like marrying and being married no longer enter into the case. Jesus was saying nothing new. In *Enoch* the promise is, "Ye shall have great joy as the angels of heaven." In the *Apocalypse of Baruch* it is said that the righteous shall be made "like unto the angels." And the rabbinic writings themselves said that in the life to come "there is no eating and drinking, no begetting of children, no bargaining, jealousy, hatred and strife, but that the righteous sit with crowns on their heads, and are satisfied with the glory of God." It is Jesus' point that the life to come cannot be thought of in terms of this life at all.

Second, he deals with the fact of the resurrection. Here he meets the Sadducees on their own ground. They insisted that in the Pentateuch, by which they set so much store, there was no evidence for immortality. From the Pentateuch Jesus draws his proof. In Exodus 3:6, God calls himself the God of Abraham, the God of Isaac and the God of Jacob. If God is the God of these patriarchs even yet, it means that they must still be alive, for the living God must be the God of living people, and not of those who are dead. And if the patriarchs are alive then the resurrection is proved.

12th Day of Lent

John 6:35–40

Jesus said to them: "I am the bread of life. He who comes to me will never hunger, and he who believes in me will never thirst any more. But I tell you, though you have seen me, yet you do not believe in me. All that the Father gives me will come to me, because I came down from heaven, not to do my will, but to do the will of him who sent me. This is the will of him who sent me—that I should lose none of those he gave to me, but that I should raise them all up on the last day. This is the will of my Father, that everyone who believes on the Son, when he sees him, should have everlasting life. And I will raise him up on the last day."

This is one of the great passages of the Fourth Gospel, and indeed of the New Testament. In it there are two great lines of thought that we must try to analyse.

First, what did Jesus mean when he said: "I am the bread of life"? It is not enough to regard this as simply a beautiful and poetical phrase. Let us analyse it step by step. (i) Bread sustains life. It is that without which life cannot go on. (ii) But what is life? Clearly by life is meant something far more than mere physical existence. What is this new spiritual meaning of life? (iii) Real life is the new relationship with God, that relationship of trust and obedience and love of which we have already thought. (iv) That relationship is made possible only by Jesus Christ. Apart from him no one can enter into it. (v) That is to say, without Jesus there may be existence, but not life. (vi) Therefore, if Jesus is the essential of life, he may be described as the bread of life. The hunger of the human situation is ended when we know Christ and through him know God. The restless soul is at rest; the hungry heart is satisfied.

Second, this passage opens out to us the stages of the Christian life. (i) We see Jesus. We see him in the pages of the New Testament, in the teaching of the church, sometimes even face to face. (ii) Having seen him, we come to him. We regard him not as some distant hero and pattern, not as a figure in a book, but as someone accessible. (iii) We believe in him. That is to say, we accept him as the final authority on God, on humanity, on life. That means that our coming is not a matter of mere interest, nor a meeting on equal terms; it is essentially a submission. (iv) This process gives us life. That is to say, it puts us into a new and lovely relationship with God, wherein he becomes an intimate friend; we are now at home with the one whom we feared or never knew. (v) The possibility of this is free and universal. The invitation is to all. The bread of life is ours for the taking. (vi) The only way to that new relationship is through Jesus. Without him it never would have been possible; and apart from him it is still impossible. No searching of the human mind or longing of the human heart can fully find God apart from Jesus. (vii) At the back of the whole process is God. It is those whom God has given him who come to Christ. God not only provides the goal; he moves in the human heart to awaken desire for him; and he works in the human heart to take away the rebellion and the pride which would hinder the great submission. We could never even have sought him unless he had already found us. (viii) There remains that stubborn something which enables us to refuse the offer of God. In the last analysis, the one thing which defeats God is the defiance of the human heart. Life is there for the taking—or the refusing.

When we take, two things happen.

First, into life enters new satisfaction. The hunger and the thirst are gone. The human heart finds what it was searching for and life ceases to be mere existence and becomes a thing at once of thrill and of peace.

Second, even beyond life we are safe. Even on the last day when all things end we are still secure. As a great commentator said: "Christ brings us to the haven beyond which there is no danger."

The offer of Christ is life in time and life in eternity. That is the greatness and glory of which we cheat ourselves when we refuse his invitation.

13th Day of Lent

John 6:51–59

"The bread which I will give him is my flesh, which is given that the world may have life." So the Jews argued with each other. "How," they said, "can this man give us his flesh to eat?" Jesus said to them: "This is the truth I tell you—unless you eat the flesh of the Son of Man and drink his blood, you cannot possess eternal life within yourselves. He who eats my flesh and drinks my blood has eternal life, and I will raise him up on

the last day. My flesh is the real food and my blood is the real drink. He who eats my flesh and drinks my blood remains in me and I in him. As the living Father has sent me, so I live through him; and he who eats me will live through me. This is the bread which came down from heaven. It is not a case of eating, as your fathers ate and died. He who eats this bread lives for ever." He said these things when he was teaching in the synagogue at Capernaum.

To most of us this is a very difficult passage. It speaks in language and moves in a world of ideas which are quite strange to us and which may seem even fantastic and grotesque. But to those who heard it first, it was moving among familiar ideas which went back to the very childhood of the race.

These ideas would be quite normal to anyone brought up in ancient sacrifice. The animal was very seldom burned entire. Usually only a token part was burned on the altar, although the whole animal was offered to the god. Part of the flesh was given to the priests as their perquisite; and part to the worshipper to make a feast for himself and his friends within the temple precincts. At that feast the god himself was held to be a guest. More, once the flesh had been offered to the god, it was held that he had entered into it; and therefore when worshippers ate it they were literally eating the god. When people rose from such a feast they went out, as they believed, literally god-filled. We may think of it as idolatrous worship, we may think of it as a vast delusion; yet the fact remains these people went out quite certain that in them there was now the dynamic vitality of their god. To people used to that kind of experience a section like this presented no difficulties at all.

It may be well that we should remember that here John is doing what he so often does. He is not giving, or trying to give, the actual words of Jesus. He has been thinking for seventy years of what Jesus said; and now, led by the Holy Spirit, he is giving the inner significance of his words. It is not the words that he reports; that would merely have been a feat of memory. It is the essential meaning of the words; that is the guidance of the Holy Spirit.

Let us see now if we can find out something of what Jesus meant and of what John understood from words like this. We may take this passage in a quite general sense. Jesus spoke about eating his flesh and drinking his blood.

Now the flesh of Jesus was his complete humanity. John in his First Letter lays it down almost passionately: "Every spirit that confesses that Jesus Christ has come in the flesh is of God; and every spirit which does not confess Jesus is not of God." In fact, the spirit which denies that Jesus is come in the flesh is of antichrist (1 John 4:2, 3). John insisted that we must grasp and never let go the full humanity of Jesus, that he was bone of our bone and flesh of our flesh. What does this mean? Jesus, as we have seen again and again, was the mind of God become a person. This means that in Jesus we see God taking human life upon him, facing our human situation, struggling with our human problems, battling with our human temptations, working out our human relationships.

Jesus said we must drink his blood. In Jewish thought the blood stands for the life. It is easy to understand why. As the blood flows from a wound, life ebbs away; and to the Jew, the blood belonged to God. That is why to this day a true Jew will never eat any meat which has not been completely drained of blood. "Only you shall not eat flesh with its life, that is, its blood" (Genesis 9:4). "Only you shall not eat its blood" (Deuteronomy 15:23). Now see what Jesus is saying— "You must drink my blood—you must take my life into the very centre of your being—and that life of mine is the life which belongs to God." When Jesus said we must drink his blood he meant that we must take his life into the very core of our hearts.

What does that mean? Think of it this way. Here in a bookcase is a book which its owner has never read. It may be the glory and the wonder of the tragedies of Shakespeare; but so long as it remains unread upon the bookshelves it is external to the one who owns it. One day it is taken down and read. The reader is thrilled and fascinated and moved. The story speaks; the great lines stick in memory. Now it belongs to the book owner, who can pull that wonder up from inside and think about it, and feed mind and heart upon it. Once the book was outside and unknown; now it is inside and can be used to feed the soul. It is that way with any great experience in life. It remains external until we take it within ourselves.

It is so with Jesus. So long as he remains a figure in a book he is external to us; but when he enters into our hearts we can feed upon the life and the strength and the dynamic vitality that he gives to us.

14th Day of Lent

John 7:37–44

On the last, the great day of the festival, Jesus stood and cried: "If anyone thirsts, let him come to me and drink. As the scripture says: 'He who believes in me—rivers of living water shall flow from his belly.'" It was about the Spirit, whom those who believed in him were to receive, that he said this. For as yet there was no Spirit because Jesus was not yet glorified. When they heard these words some of the crowd said: "This is really the promised Prophet." Others said: "This is the Anointed One of God." But some said: "Surely the Anointed One of God does not come from Galilee? Does the scripture not say that the Anointed One of God is a descendant of David, and that he is to come from Bethlehem, the village where David used to live?" So there was a division of opinion in the crowd because of him. Some of them would have liked to arrest him, but none laid hands on him.

The promise of Jesus presents us with something of a problem. He said: "He who believes in me—rivers of water shall flow from his belly." And he introduces that statement by saying, "as scripture says." No one has ever been able to identify that quotation satisfactorily, and the question is, just what does it mean? There are two distinct possibilities.

(i) It may refer to those who come to Jesus and accept him. They will have within them a river of refreshing water. It would be another way of saying what Jesus said to the woman of Samaria: "The water that I shall give him will become in him a spring of water welling up to eternal life" (John 4:14). It would be another way of putting Isaiah's beautiful saying: "And the Lord will guide you continually, and satisfy your desire with good things, and make your bones strong; and you shall be like a watered garden, like a spring of water, whose waters fail not" (Isaiah 58:11). The meaning would be that Jesus can give a person the refreshment of the Holy Spirit.

The Jews placed all the thoughts and the emotions in certain parts of the body. The heart was the seat of the intellect; the kidneys and the belly were the seat of the inmost feelings. As the writer of the Proverbs had it: "The spirit of man is the lamp of the Lord, searching all his innermost parts" (Proverbs 20:27). This would mean that Jesus was promising a cleansing, refreshing, life-giving stream of the Holy Spirit so that our thoughts and feelings would be purified and revitalised. It is as if Jesus said: "Come to me and accept me; and I will put into you through my Spirit a new life which will give you purity and satisfaction, and give you the kind of life you have always longed for and never had." Whichever interpretation we take, it is quite certain that what this one stands for is true.

(ii) The other interpretation is that "rivers of living water shall flow from his belly" may refer to Jesus himself. It may be a description of the Messiah which Jesus is taking from somewhere which we cannot place. The Christians always identified Jesus with the rock which gave the Israelites water in the wilderness (Exodus 17:6). Paul took that image and applied it to Christ (1 Corinthians 10:4). John tells how there came forth at the thrust of the soldier's spear water and blood from Jesus' side (John 19:34). The water stands for the purification which comes in baptism and the blood for the atoning death of the cross. This symbol of the life-giving water which comes from God is often in the Old Testament (Psalm 105:41; Ezekiel 47:1, 12). Joel has the great picture: "And a fountain shall come forth from the house of the Lord" (Joel 3:18). It may well be that John is thinking of Jesus as the fountain from which the cleansing stream flows. Water is that without which man cannot live; and Christ is the one without whom man cannot live and dare not die. Again, whichever interpretation we choose, that, too, is deeply true.

Whether we take this picture as referring to Christ or to the one who accepts him, it means that from Christ there flows the strength and power and cleansing which alone give us life in the real sense of the term.

In this passage there is a startling thing. The Authorized Version and the Revised Standard tone it down, but in the best Greek manuscript there is the strange statement in verse 39: "For as yet there was no Spirit." What is the meaning of that? Think of it this way. A great power can exist for years and even centuries without our being able to tap it. To take a very relevant example—there has always been atomic power in this world; we did not invent it. But only in our own time have scientists tapped and used it. The Holy Spirit has always existed; but people never really enjoyed his full power until after Pentecost. As it has been finely said, "There could be no Pentecost without Calvary." It was only when people had known Jesus that they really knew the Spirit. Before that the Spirit had been a power, but now the Spirit is known as a person who has become to us nothing other than the presence of the Risen Christ, always with us. In this apparently startling sentence John is not saying that the Spirit did not exist; but that it took the life and death of Jesus Christ to open the floodgates for the Spirit to become real and powerful to all.

15th Day of Lent

John 10:16

"But I have other sheep which are not of this fold. These too I must bring in, and they will hear my voice; and they will become one flock, and there will be one shepherd."

One of the hardest things in the world to unlearn is exclusiveness. Once a people, or a section of a people, gets the idea that they are specially privileged, it is very difficult for them to accept that the privileges which they believed belonged to them and to them only are in fact open to all. That is what the Jews never learned. They believed that they were God's chosen people and that God had no use for any other nation. They believed that, at the best, other nations were designed to be their slaves, and, at the worst, that they were destined for elimination from the scheme of things. But here Jesus is saying that there will come a day when all will know him as their shepherd.

Even the Old Testament is not without its glimpses of that day. Isaiah had that very dream. It was his conviction that God had given Israel for "a light to the nations" (Isaiah 42:6; 49:6; 56:8) and always there had been some lonely voices which insisted that God was not the exclusive property of Israel, but that the nation's destiny was to make him known to all people. At first sight it might seem that the New Testament speaks with two voices on this subject; and some passages of the New Testament may well trouble and perplex us a little. As Matthew tells the story, when Jesus sent out his disciples, he said to them: "Go nowhere among the Gentiles, and enter no town of the Samaritans, but go rather to the lost sheep of the house of Israel" (Matthew 10:5, 6). When the Syro-Phoenician woman appealed to Jesus for help, his first answer was that he was sent only to the lost sheep of the house of Israel (Matthew 15:24). But there is much to be set on the other side. Jesus himself stayed and taught in Samaria (John 4:40); he declared that descent from Abraham was no guarantee of entry into the kingdom (John 8:39). It was of a Roman centurion that Jesus said that he had never seen such faith in Israel (Matthew 8:10); it was a Samaritan leper who alone returned to give thanks (Luke 17:18, 19); it was the Samaritan traveler who showed the kindness that all disciples must copy (Luke 10:37); many would come from the east and the west and the north and the south to sit down in the Kingdom of God (Matthew 8:11; Luke 13:29); the command in the end was to go out and to preach the gospel to all nations (Mark 16:15; Matthew 28:19); Jesus was, not the light of the Jews, but the light of the world (John 8:12).

What is the explanation of the sayings which seem to limit the work of Jesus to the Jews? The explanation is in reality very simple. The ultimate aim of Jesus was the world for God. But any great commander knows that you must in the first instance limit your objectives. If you try to attack on too wide a front, you only scatter your forces, diffuse your strength, and gain success nowhere. In order to win an ultimately complete victory you must begin by concentrating your forces at certain limited objectives. That is what Jesus did. Had he gone here, there and everywhere, had he sent his disciples out with no limitation to their sphere of work, nothing would have been achieved. At the moment he deliberately concentrated on the Jewish nation, but his ultimate aim was the gathering of the whole world into his love.

The only possible unity for all people is in their common relationship with God. In the world there is division between nation and nation; in the nation there is division between class and class. There can never be one nation; and there can never be one class. The only thing which can cross the barriers and wipe out the distinctions is the gospel of Jesus Christ telling all people of the universal love of God.

In the Authorized Version there is a mistranslation. It has: "There shall be one fold and one shepherd." That mistranslation goes back to Jerome and the Vulgate. And on that mistranslation the Roman Catholic Church has based the teaching that, since there is only one fold, there can only be one church, the Roman Catholic Church, and that, outside it there is no salvation. But the real translation beyond all possible doubt as given in the Revised Standard Version, is: "There shall be one flock, one shepherd," or, even better, "They shall become one flock and there shall be one shepherd." The unity comes from the fact, not that all the sheep are forced into one fold, but they all hear, answer and obey one shepherd. It is not an ecclesiastical unity; it is a unity of loyalty to Jesus Christ. The fact that there is one flock does not mean that there can be only one church, one method of worship, one form of ecclesiastical administration. But it does mean that all the different churches are united by a common loyalty to Jesus Christ.

But this saying of Jesus becomes very personal; for it is a dream which every one of us can help Jesus to realize. People cannot hear without a preacher; the other sheep cannot be gathered in unless someone goes out to bring them in. Here is set before us the tremendous missionary task of the church. And we must not think of that only in terms of what we used to call foreign missions. If we know persons here and now who do not know God's love, we can tell them of Christ. The dream of Christ depends on us; it is we who can help make the world one flock with him as its shepherd.

16th Day of Lent

Matthew 24:32–41

"Learn the lesson which comes from the fig tree. Whenever the branch has become tender, and puts forth its leaves, you know that summer is near. Even so, when you too see these things, know that he is near at the doors. This is the truth I tell you—this generation shall not pass away, until these things have happened. Heaven and earth will pass away, but my words will not pass away.

No one knows about that day and hour, not even the angels of heaven, not even the Son, but only the Father. As were the days of Noah, so will be the coming of the Son of Man. For, as in those days before the flood they spent their time eating and drinking, marrying and giving in marriage, until the day that Noah entered into the ark, and were quite unaware of what was to happen until the flood came and swept them all away, so will be the coming of the Son of Man. At that time there will be two men in the field; one is taken, and the other is left. There will be two women grinding with the mill; one is taken, and the other is left."

Few passages confront us with greater difficulties than this. It is in two sections and they seem to contradict each other.

The first (verses 32–35) seems to indicate that, as we can tell by the signs of nature when summer is on the way, so we can tell by the signs of the world when the Second Coming is on the way. Then it seems to go on to say that the Second Coming will happen within the lifetime of the generation listening to Jesus at that moment.

The second section (verses 36–41) says quite definitely that no one knows the time of the Second Coming, not the angels, not even Jesus himself, but only God; and that it will come upon the world with the suddenness of a rainstorm out of a blue sky.

There is a very real difficulty here which, even if we cannot completely solve, we must nevertheless boldly face. Let us take as our starting-point verse 34: "This is the truth I tell you—this generation shall not pass away, until these things have happened." When we consider that saying, three possibilities emerge.

(a) If Jesus said it in reference to the Second Coming, he was mistaken for he did not return within the lifetime of the generation listening to his words. Many accept that point of view, believing that Jesus in his humanity had limitations of knowledge and did believe that within that generation he would return. We can readily accept that in his humanity Jesus had limitations of knowledge; but it is difficult to believe that he was in error regarding so great a spiritual truth as this.

(b) It is possible that Jesus said something like this which was changed in the transmitting. In Mark 9:1 Jesus is reported as saying, "Truly I say to you, there are some standing here who will not taste death before they see the Kingdom of God come with power." That was gloriously and triumphantly true. Within that generation the Kingdom of God did spread mightily until there were Christians throughout the known world.

Now the early Christians did look for the Second Coming immediately. In their situation of suffering and persecution they looked and longed for the release that the coming of their Lord would bring, and sometimes they took sayings which were intended to speak of the Kingdom and attached them to the Second Coming which is a very different thing. Something like that may have happened here. What Jesus may have said was that his kingdom would come mightily before that generation had passed away.

(c) But there is a third possibility. What if the phrase "until these things have happened" has no reference to the Second Coming? What if their reference is, in fact, to the prophecy with which the chapter began, the siege and fall of Jerusalem? If we accept that, there is no difficulty. What Jesus is saying is that these grim warnings of his regarding the doom of Jerusalem will be fulfilled within that very generation—and they were, in fact, fulfilled forty years later. It seems by far the best course to take verses 32–35 as referring, not to the Second Coming, but to the doom of Jerusalem, for then all the difficulties in them are removed.

Verses 36–41 do refer to the Second Coming; and they tell us certain most important truths.

(i) They tell us that the hour of that event is known to God and to God alone. It is, therefore, clear that speculation regarding the time of the Second Coming is nothing less than blasphemy, for the one who so speculates is seeking to wrest from God secrets which belong to God alone. It is not any one's duty to speculate; it is each one's duty to prepare, and to watch.

(ii) They tell us that that time will come with shattering suddenness on those who are immersed in material things. In the old story Noah prepared in the calm weather for the flood which was to come, and when it came he was ready. But the rest of mankind were lost in their eating and drinking and marrying and giving in marriage, and were caught completely unawares, and were therefore swept away. These verses are a warning never to become so immersed in time that we forget eternity, never to let our concern with worldly affairs, however necessary, completely distract us from remembering that there is a God, that the issues of life and death are in God's hands, and that whenever the call comes, at morning, at midday, or at evening, it must find us ready.

(iii) They tell us that the coming of Christ will be a time of separation and of judgment, when he will gather to himself those who are his own.

Beyond these things we cannot go—for God has kept the ultimate knowledge to himself and his wisdom.

Third Sunday in Lent

John 2:14–22

In the Temple he found those who were selling oxen and sheep and doves, and the money-changers sitting at their tables. He made a scourge of cords and drove them all out of the Temple, and the sheep and the oxen as well. He scattered the coins of the exchangers and overturned their tables. He said to those who were selling doves: "Take these away and stop making my Father's house a house of trade." His disciples remembered that there is a scripture which stands written: "For zeal for your house has consumed me." Then the Jews demanded of him: "What sign do you show us to justify your acting in this way?" Jesus answered: "Destroy this Temple and in three days I will raise it up." Then the Jews said: "It has taken forty-six years to build the Temple so far, and are you going to raise it up in three days?" But he was speaking about the temple of his body. So when he was raised from the dead, his disciples remembered that he had said this, and they believed on the scripture and on the word which Jesus spoke.

It was quite certain that an act like the cleansing of the Temple would produce an immediate reaction in those who saw it happening. It was not the kind of thing that anyone could look at with complete indifference. It was much too staggering for that.

Here we have two reactions. First, there is the reaction of the disciples which was to remember the words of Psalm 69:9. The point is that this Psalm was taken to refer to the Messiah. When the Messiah came he would be burned up with a zeal for the house of God. When this verse leapt into their minds, it meant the conviction that Jesus was the Messiah seized the minds of the disciples even more deeply and more definitely. This action befitted none but the Messiah, and they were surer than ever that Jesus was in fact the Anointed One of God.

Second, there is the reaction of the Jews, a very natural one. They asked what right Jesus had to act like that and demanded that he should at once prove his credentials by some sign. The point is this. They acknowledged the act of Jesus to be that of one who thereby claimed to be the Messiah. It was always expected that when the Messiah came he would confirm his claims by doing amazing things. False Messiahs did in fact arise and promise to cleave the waters of Jordan in two or make the walls of the city collapse at a word. The popular idea of the Messiah was connected with wonders. So the Jews said: "By this act of yours you have publicly claimed to be the Messiah. Now show us some wonder which will prove your claim."

Jesus' reply constitutes the great problem of this passage. What did he really say? And what did he really mean? It is always to be remembered that verses 21 and 22 are John's interpretation written long afterwards. He was inevitably reading into the passage ideas which were the product of seventy years of thinking about and experience of the

Risen Christ. As Irenaeus said long ago: "No prophecy is fully understood until after the fulfillment of it." But what did Jesus originally say and what did he originally mean?

There is no possible doubt that Jesus spoke words which were very like these, words which could be maliciously twisted into a destructive claim. When Jesus was on trial, the false witness borne against him was: "This fellow said, I am able to destroy the temple of God, and to build it in three days" (Matthew 26:61). The charge levelled against Stephen was: "We have heard him say that this Jesus of Nazareth will destroy this place, and will change the customs which Moses delivered to us" (Acts 6:14).

We must remember two things and we must put them together. First, Jesus certainly never said he would destroy the material Temple and then rebuild it. Jesus in fact looked for the end of the Temple. He said to the woman of Samaria that the day was coming when people would worship God neither in Mount Gerizim, nor in Jerusalem, but in spirit and in truth (John 4:21). Second, the cleansing of the Temple, as we have seen, was a dramatic way of showing that the whole Temple worship with its ritual and its sacrifice was irrelevant and could do nothing to lead the people to God. It is clear that Jesus did expect that the Temple would pass away; that he had come to render its worship unnecessary and obsolete; and that therefore he would never suggest that he would rebuild it.

We must now turn to Mark. As so often, we find the little extra suggestive and illuminating phrase there. As Mark relates the charge against Jesus, it ran: "I will destroy this Temple that is made with hands, and in three days I will build another not made with hands" (Mark 14:58). What Jesus really meant was that his coming had put an end to all this ritualistic way of worshipping God and put in its place a spiritual worship; that he put an end to all this business of animal sacrifice and priestly ritual and put in its place a direct approach to the Spirit of God which did not need an elaborate Temple made with human hands and a ritual of incense and sacrifice offered by humans. The threat of Jesus was: "Your Temple worship, your elaborate ritual, your lavish animal sacrifices are at an end, because I have come." The promise of Jesus was: "I will give you a way to come to God without all this human elaboration and human ritual. I have come to destroy this Temple in Jerusalem and to make the whole earth the Temple where everyone can know the presence of the living God."

We have here the tremendous truth that our contact with God, our entry into God's presence, our approach to God is not dependent on anything that human hands can build or human minds devise. In the street, in the home, at business, on the hills, on the open road, in church we have our inner temple, the presence of the Risen Christ for ever with us throughout all the world.

17th Day of Lent

Mark 2:1–6

When, some time afterwards, Jesus had come back to Capernaum, the news went round that he was in a house. Such crowds collected that there was no longer any room left, not even round the door. So he was speaking the word to them. A party arrived bringing to him a paralysed man carried by four men. When they could not get near him because of the crowd they unroofed part of the roof of the house in which he was, and when they had dug out part of the roof, they let down the stretcher on which the paralysed man was lying. When Jesus saw their faith, he said to the paralysed man, "Child, your sins are forgiven." Some of the experts in the law were sitting there, and they were debating within themselves, "How can this fellow speak like this? He is insulting God. Who can forgive sins except one person—God?" Jesus immediately knew in his spirit that this debate was going on in their minds, so he said to them, "Why do you debate thus in your minds? Which is easier—to say to the paralysed man, 'Your sins are forgiven,' or to say, 'Get up, and lift your bed, and walk around'? Just to let you see that the Son of Man has authority on earth to forgive sins"—he said to the paralysed man—"I say to you, 'Get up! Lift your bed! And go away home!'" And he raised himself, and immediately he lifted his bed, and went out in front of them all. The result was that they were all astonished, and they kept on praising God. "Never," they kept repeating, "have we seen anything like this."

Jesus, as we have seen, had already attracted the crowds. Because of that he had attracted the notice of the official leaders of the Jews. The Sanhedrin was their supreme court. One of its great functions was to be the guardian of orthodoxy. For instance, it was the Sanhedrin's duty to deal with anyone who was a false prophet. It seems that it had sent out a kind of scouting party to check up on Jesus; and they were there in Capernaum. No doubt they had annexed an honourable place in the front of the crowd and were sitting there critically watching everything that was going on.

When they heard Jesus say to the man that his sins were forgiven it came as a shattering shock. It was an essential of the Jewish faith that only God could forgive sins. For any human to claim to do so was to insult God; that was blasphemy and the penalty for blasphemy was death by stoning (Leviticus 24:16). At the moment they were not ready to launch their attack in public, but it was not difficult for Jesus to see how their minds were working. So he determined to fling down a challenge and to meet them on their own ground.

It was their own firm belief that sin and sickness were indissolubly linked together. A sick person was a person who had sinned. So Jesus asked them: "Whether it is easier to say to this man, 'Your sins are forgiven,' or to say, 'Get up and walk'?" Any charlatan could say, "Your sins are forgiven." There was no possibility of ever demonstrating whether the words were effective; such a statement was completely uncheckable. But to say, "Get up and walk" was to say something whose effectiveness would either be proved or disproved there and then. So Jesus said in effect: "You say that I have no right to forgive sins? You hold as a matter of belief that if this man is ill he is a sinner and he cannot be cured till he is forgiven? Very well, then, watch this!" So Jesus spoke the word and the man was cured.

The experts in the law were hoist with their own petard. On their own stated beliefs the man could not be cured, unless he was forgiven. He was cured, therefore he was forgiven. Therefore, Jesus' claim to forgive sin must be true. Jesus must have left a completely baffled set of legal experts; and, worse, he must have left them in a baffled rage. Here was something that must be dealt with; if this went on, all orthodox religion would be shattered and destroyed. In this incident Jesus signed his own death warrant—and he knew it.

For all that it is an extremely difficult incident. What does it mean that Jesus can forgive sin? There are three possible ways of looking at this.

(i) We could take it that Jesus was conveying God's forgiveness to the man. After David had sinned and Nathan had rebuked him into terror and David had humbly confessed his sin, Nathan said: "The Lord also has put away your sin; you shall not die" (2 Samuel 12:1–13). Nathan was not forgiving David's sin, but he was conveying God's forgiveness to David and assuring him of it. So we could say that what Jesus was doing was that he was assuring the man of God's forgiveness, conveying to him something which God had already given him. That is certainly true, but it does not read as if it was the whole truth.

(ii) We could take it that Jesus was acting as God's representative. John says: "The Father judges no one, but has given all judgment to the Son" (John 5:22). If judgment is committed to Jesus, then so must forgiveness be. Let us take a human analogy. Analogies are always imperfect but we can think only in human terms. One person may give another a "power of attorney"; that means to say that one has given to another the absolute disposal of his or her goods and property. It is an agreeement that another should act for the property owner, and that those actions should be regarded precisely as the owner's own actions. We could take it that that is what God did with Jesus—delegated to him God's own powers and privileges, and that the word Jesus spoke was none other than the word of God.

(iii) We could take it in still another way. The whole essence of Jesus' life is that in him we see clearly displayed the attitude of God to all humankind. Now that attitude was the very reverse of what people had thought God's attitude to be. It was not an attitude of stern, severe, austere justice, not an attitude of continual demand. It was an attitude of perfect love, of a heart yearning with love and eager to forgive. . . . Jesus showed perfectly the attitude of God to people. He could say, "I forgive," because in him God was saying, "I forgive."

18th Day of Lent

John 7:10–13

When his brothers had gone up to the festival, then he too went up, not openly, but, as it were, in secret. So the Jews searched for him at the festival, and kept saying: "Where is he?" And there was many a heated argument about him among the crowds. Some said: "He is a good man." But others said: "No; far from it; he is leading the people astray." But no one spoke about him openly because of their fear of the Jews.

Jesus chose his own moment and went to Jerusalem. Here we have the reactions of the people when they were confronted with him. Now one of the supreme interests of this chapter is the number of such reactions of which it tells; and we collect them all here.

(i) There was the reaction of his brothers (verses 1–5). It was really a reaction of half-amused and teasing contempt. They did not really believe in him; they were really egging him on, as you might egg on a precocious boy. We still meet that attitude of tolerant contempt to Christianity.

Georges Bernanos in *The Diary of a Country Priest* tells how the country priest used sometimes to be invited to dinner at the big aristocratic house of his parish. The owner would encourage him to speak and argue before his guests, but he did it with that half-amused, half-contemptuous tolerance with which he might encourage a child to show off or a dog to display his tricks. There are still people who forget that Christian faith is a matter of life and death.

(ii) There was the sheer hatred of the Pharisees and of the chief priests (verses 7, 19). They did not hate him for the same reason, because in point of fact they hated each other. The Pharisees hated him because he drove through their petty rules and regulations. If he was right, they were wrong; and they loved their own little system more than they loved God. The Sadducees were a political party. They did not observe the Pharisaic rules and regulations. Nearly all the priests were Sadducees. They collaborated with their Roman masters, and they had a very comfortable and even luxurious time. They did not want a Messiah; for when he came their political set-up would disintegrate and their comfort would be gone. They hated Jesus because he interfered with the vested interests which were dearer to them than God.

It is still possible for us to love our own little systems more than we love God, and to place our own vested interests above the challenge of the adventurous and the sacrificial way.

(iii) Both these reactions issued in the consuming desire to eliminate Jesus (verses 30, 32). When one's ideals clash with those of Christ, either one must submit or one must seek to destroy him. Hitler would have no Christians about him, for the Christian owed a higher loyalty than loyalty to the state. People are faced with a simple alternative if they allow Christ into their orbits. They can either do what they like or they can do what Christ likes; and if they wish to go on doing as they like, they must seek to eliminate Christ.

(iv) There was arrogant contempt (verses 15, 47–49). What right had this man to come and lay down the law? Jesus had no cultural background; he had no training in the rabbinic schools and colleges. Surely no intelligent person was going to listen to him? Here was the reaction of academic snobbery.

Many of the greatest poets and writers and evangelists have had no technical qualifications at all. That is not for one moment to say that study and culture and education are to be despised and abandoned; but we must have a care never to wave people away and consign them to the company of those who do not matter simply because they lack the technical equipment of the schools.

(v) There was the reaction of the crowd. This was twofold. First, there was the reaction of interest (verse 11). The one thing impossible when Jesus really invades life is indifference. Apart from anything else, Jesus is the most interesting figure in the world. Second, there was the reaction of discussion (verses 12, 43). They talked about Jesus; they put forward their views about him; they debated about him. There is both value and danger here. The value is that nothing helps us clarify our own opinions like pitting them against someone else's. Mind sharpens mind as iron sharpens iron. The danger is that religion can so very easily come to be regarded as a matter for argument and debate and discussion, a series of fascinating questions, about which people may talk for a lifetime—and do nothing. There is all the difference in the world between being an argumentative amateur theologian, willing to talk until the stars go out, and a truly religious person, who has passed from talking about Christ to knowing him.

19th Day of Lent

John 8:56–59

"Abraham your father rejoiced to see my day; and he saw it and was glad." The Jews said to him: "You are not yet fifty years old, and have you seen Abraham?" Jesus said to them: "This is the truth I tell you—before Abraham was, I am." So they lifted stones to throw them at him, but Jesus slipped out of their sight, and went out of the Temple precincts.

All the previous lightning flashes pale into insignificance before the blaze of this passage. When Jesus said to the Jews that Abraham rejoiced to see his day, he was talking language that they could understand. The Jews had many beliefs about Abraham which would enable them to see what Jesus was implying. There were altogether five different ways in which they would interpret this passage.

(a) Abraham was living in Paradise and able to see what was happening on earth. Jesus used that idea in the Parable of Dives and Lazarus (Luke 16:22–31). That is the simplest way to interpret this saying.

(b) But that is not the correct interpretation. Jesus said Abraham rejoiced to see my day, the past tense. The Jews interpreted many passages of scripture in a way that explains this. They took the great promise to Abraham in Genesis 12:3: "By you all the families of the earth shall bless themselves," and said that when that promise was made, Abraham knew that it meant that the Messiah of God was to come from his line and rejoiced at the magnificence of the promise.

(c) Some of the rabbis held that in Genesis 15:8–21 Abraham was given a vision of the whole future of the nation of Israel and therefore had a vision beforehand of the time when the Messiah would come.

(d) Some of the rabbis took Genesis 17:17, which tells how Abraham laughed when he heard that a son would be born to him, not as a laugh of unbelief, but as a laugh of sheer joy that from him the Messiah would come.

(e) Some of the rabbis had a fanciful interpretation of Genesis 24:1. There the Revised Standard Version has it that Abraham was "well advanced in years." The margin of the Authorised Version tells us that the Hebrew literally means that Abraham had "gone into days." Some of the rabbis held that to mean that in a vision given by God Abraham had "entered into the days which lay ahead," and had seen the whole history of the people and the coming of the Messiah.

From all this we see clearly that the Jews did believe that somehow Abraham, while he was still alive, had a vision of the history of Israel and the coming of the Messiah. So when Jesus said that Abraham had seen his day, he was making a deliberate claim that he was the Messiah. He was really saying: "I am the Messiah Abraham saw in his vision."

Immediately Jesus goes on to say of Abraham: "He saw it (my day) and was glad." Some of the early Christians had a very fanciful interpretation of that. In 1 Peter 3:18–22 and 4:6 we have the two passages which are the basis of that doctrine which became imbedded in the creed in the phrase, "He descended into Hell." It is to be noted that the word "Hell" gives the wrong idea; it ought to be "Hades." The idea is not that Jesus went to the place of the tortured and the damned, as the word Hell suggests. Hades was the land of the shadows where all the dead, good and bad alike, went; in which the Jews believed before the full belief in immortality came to them. The apocryphal work called *The Gospel of Nicodemus* or *The Acts of Pilate* has a passage which runs: "O Lord Jesus Christ, the resurrection and the life of the world, give us grace that we may tell of thy resurrection and of thy marvellous works, which thou didst in Hades. We, then, were in Hades together with all them that have fallen asleep since the beginning. And at the hour of midnight there rose upon those dark places as it were the light of the sun, and shined, and all we were enlightened and beheld one another. And straightway our father Abraham, together with the patriarchs and the prophets, were at once filled

with joy and said to one another: 'This light cometh of the great light-
ening.' " The dead saw Jesus and were given the chance to believe and
to repent; and at that sight Abraham rejoiced.

To us these ideas are strange; to the Jews they were quite normal,
for they believed that Abraham had already seen the day when the
Messiah would come.

The Jews, although they knew better, chose to take this literally.
"How," they demanded, "can you have seen Abraham when you are
not yet fifty?" Why fifty? That was the age at which the Levites retired
from their service (Numbers 4:3). The Jews were saying to Jesus: "You
are a young man, still in the prime of life, not even old enough to re-
tire from service. How can you possibly have seen Abraham? This is
mad talk." It was then that Jesus made that most staggering statement:
"Before Abraham was, I am." We must note carefully that Jesus did
not say: "Before Abraham was, I was," but, "Before Abraham was, I
am." Here is the claim that Jesus is timeless. There never was a time
when he came into being; there never will be a time when he is not
in being.

What did he mean? Obviously he did not mean that he, the human figure Jesus, had always existed. We know that Jesus was born
into this world at Bethlehem; there is more than that here. Think of
it this way. There is only one person in the universe who is timeless;
and that one person is God. What Jesus is saying here is nothing less
than that the life in him is the life of God; he is saying, as the writer
of the Hebrews put it more simply, that he is the same yesterday, today and forever. In Jesus we see, not simply a person who came and
lived and died; we see the timeless God, who was the God of Abraham and of Isaac and of Jacob, who was before time and who will be
after time, who always is. In Jesus the eternal God showed himself to
all humankind.

20th Day of Lent

Matthew 21:33–41

*Jesus said, "Listen to another parable. There was a householder who
planted a vineyard, and surrounded it with a hedge, and dug a wine press*

*in it, and built a tower, and gave it out to cultivators and went away.
When the time of the fruits had come, he dispatched his servants to the
cultivators, to receive his fruits; and the cultivators took his servants, and
beat one of them, and killed another of them, and stoned another of them.
Again he dispatched other servants, more than the first; and they did the
same to them. Afterwards he dispatched his son to them. 'They will respect my son,' he said. But when the cultivators saw the son, they said to
themselves, 'This is the heir. Come, let us kill him, and let us take the in-
heritance.' And they threw him out of the vineyard and killed him. When
the owner of the vineyard comes, what will he do to these cultivators?"
They said to him, "He will bring these evil men to an evil end, and he
will give out the vineyard to other cultivators, who will pay him the fruits
at their correct time."*

When the chief priests and Pharisees heard his parables, they knew
that he was speaking about them. They tried to find a way to lay hold
on him, but they were afraid of the crowds, for they regarded him as
a prophet.

In interpreting a parable it is normally a first principle that every
parable has only one point and that the details are not to be stressed.
Normally to try to find a meaning for every detail is to make the mistake of treating the parable as an allegory. But in this case it is different. In this parable the details do have a meaning and the chief priests
and the Pharisees well knew what Jesus was meaning this parable to
say to them.

Before we treat it in detail, let us set these identifications down.
The vineyard is the nation of Israel, and its owner is God. The cultivators are the religious leaders of Israel, who as it were had charge for
God of the welfare of the nation. The messengers who were sent suc-
cessively are the prophets sent by God and so often rejected and killed.
The son who came last is none other than Jesus himself. Here in a
vivid story Jesus set out at one and the same time the history and the
doom of Israel.

This parable has much to tell us in three directions.

(i) It has much to tell us about God.

(a) It tells of God's trust in us. The owner of the vineyard entrusted it to the cultivators. He did not even stand over them to exercise a police-like supervision. He went away and left them with their task. God pays us the compliment of entrusting us with his work. Every task we receive is a task given us to do by God.

(b) It tells of God's patience. The master sent messenger after messenger. He did not come with sudden vengeance when one messenger had been abused and ill-treated. He gave the cultivators chance after chance to respond to his appeal. God bears with people in all their sinning and will not cast them off.

(c) It tells of God's judgment. In the end the master of the vineyard took the vineyard from the cultivators and gave it to others. God's sternest judgment is when he takes out of our hands the task which we were meant to do. People have sunk to their lowest level when they have become useless to God.

(ii) It has much to tell us about humanity.

(a) It tells of human privilege. The vineyard was equipped with everything—the hedge, the wine press, the tower—which would make the task of the cultivators easy and enable them to discharge it well. God does not only give us a task to do, but also the means whereby to do it.

(b) It tells of human freedom. The master left the cultivators to do the task as they liked. God is no tyrannical task-master, but a wise executive who allocates a task and then trusts the person assigned to do it.

(c) It tells of human answerability. To all people comes a day of reckoning. We are answerable for the way in which we have carried out the task God gave us to do.

(d) It tells of the deliberateness of human sin. The cultivators carry out a deliberate policy of rebellion and disobedience towards the master. Sin is deliberate opposite to God; it is the taking of our own way when we know quite well what the way of God is.

(iii) It has much to tell us about Jesus.

(a) It tells of the claim of Jesus. It shows us quite clearly Jesus lifting himself out of the succession of the prophets. Those who come before him were the messengers of God; no one could deny them that honour; but they were servants; he was the Son. This parable contains one of the clearest claims Jesus ever made to be unique, to be different from even the greatest of those who went before.

(b) It tells of the sacrifice of Jesus. It makes it clear that Jesus knew what lay ahead. In the parable wicked people killed the son. Jesus was never in any doubt of what lay ahead. He did not die because he was compelled to die; he went open-eyed to death.

21st Day of Lent

Luke 5:16, 17
Jesus withdrew into the desert places and he continued in prayer. On a certain day he was teaching and, sitting listening, there were Pharisees and experts in the law who had come from every village in Galilee and from Judaea and Jerusalem. And the power of the Lord was there to enable him to heal.

There are only two verses here; but as we read them we must pause, for this indeed is a milestone. The scribes and the Pharisees had arrived on the scene. The opposition which would never be satisfied until it had killed Jesus had emerged into the open.

If we are to understand what happened to Jesus we must understand something about the Law, and the relationship of the scribes and the Pharisees to it. When the Jews returned from Babylon about 440 B.C. they knew well that, humanly speaking, their hopes of national greatness were gone. They therefore deliberately decided that they would find their greatness in being a people of the law. They would bend all their energies to knowing and keeping God's law.

The basis of the law was the Ten Commandments. These commandments are principles for life. They are not rules and regulations; they do not legislate for each event and for every circumstance. For a certain section of the Jews that was not enough. They desired not great principles but a rule to cover every conceivable situation. From the Ten Commandments they proceeded to develop and elaborate these rules.

Let us take an example. The commandment says, "Remember the Sabbath day to keep it holy"; and then goes on to lay it down that on the Sabbath no work must be done (Exodus 20:8–11). But the Jews asked, "What is work?" and went on to define it under thirty-nine different heads which they called "Fathers of Work." Even that was not enough. Each of these heads was greatly sub-divided. Thousands of rules and regulations began to emerge. These were called the Oral Law, and they began to be set even above the Ten Commandments.

Again, let us take an actual example. One of the works forbidden on the Sabbath was carrying a burden. Jeremiah 17:21–24 says, "Take heed for the sake of your lives, and do not bear a burden on the Sabbath day." But, the legalists insisted, a burden must be defined. So definition was given. A burden is "food equal in weight to a dried fig, enough wine for mixing in a goblet, milk enough for one swallow, oil enough to anoint a small member, water enough to moisten an eye-salve, paper enough to write a custom-house notice upon, ink enough to write two letters, reed enough to make a pen" . . . and so on endlessly. So for a tailor to leave a pin or needle in his robe on the Sabbath was to break the law and to sin; to pick up a stone big enough to fling at a bird on the Sabbath was to sin. Goodness became identified with these endless rules and regulations.

Let us take another example. To heal on the Sabbath was to work. It was laid down that only if life was in actual danger could healing be done; and then steps could be taken only to keep the sufferer from getting worse, not to improve his condition. A plain bandage could be put on a wound, but not any ointment; plain wadding could be put into a sore ear, but not medicated. It is easy to see that there was no limit to this.

The scribes were the experts in the law who knew all these rules and regulations, and who deduced them from the law. The name Pharisee means "The Separated One"; and the Pharisees were those who had separated themselves from ordinary people and ordinary life in order to keep these rules and regulations. Note two things. First, for the scribes and Pharisees these rules were a matter of life and death; to break one of them was deadly sin. Second, only people desperately in earnest would ever have tried to keep them, for they must have made life supremely uncomfortable. It was only the best people who would even make the attempt.

Jesus had no use for rules and regulations like that. For him, the cry of human need superseded all such things. But to the scribes and Pharisees he was a law-breaker, a bad man who broke the law and taught others to do the same. That is why they hated him and in the end killed him. The tragedy of the life of Jesus was that those who were most in earnest about their religion drove him to the cross. It was the irony of things that the best people of the day ultimately crucified him.

From this time on there was to be no rest for him. Always he was to be under the scrutiny of hostile and critical eyes. The opposition had crystallized and there was but one end.

Jesus knew this and before he met the opposition he withdrew to pray. The love in the eyes of God compensated him for the hate in the eyes of his persecutors. The approval of God nerved him to meet the criticism of his enemies. He drew strength for the battle of life from the peace of God—and it is enough for the disciple that he should be as his Lord.

22nd Day of Lent

Matthew 23:13, 15

"Alas for you, scribes and Pharisees, hypocrites, for you shut the door to the Kingdom of Heaven in the face of men! You yourselves are not going into it; nor do you allow those who are trying to get into it to enter it."
. . . "Alas for you, scribes and Pharisees, for you range over the sea and the dry land to make one proselyte, and, when that happens, you make him twice as much a son of hell as yourselves!"

Verses 13–26 of this chapter form the most terrible and the most sustained denunciation in the New Testament. Here we hear what A. T. Robertson called "the rolling thunder of Christ's wrath." As Plummer has written, these woes are "like thunder in their unanswerable severity, and like lightning in their unsparing exposure. . . . They illuminate while they strike."

Here Jesus directs a series of seven woes against the scribes and Pharisees. The Revised Standard Version begins every one of them: "Woe to you!" The Greek word for "woe" is *ouai;* it is hard to translate for it includes not only wrath, but also sorrow. There is righteous anger here, but it is the anger of the heart of love, broken by stubborn blindness. There is not only an air of savage denunciation; there is also an atmosphere of poignant tragedy.

The word "hypocrite" occurs here again and again. Originally the Greek word *hupokrites* meant "one who answers"; it then came to be specially connected with the statement and answer, the dialogue, of the stage; and it is the regular Greek word for an actor. It then came to mean an actor in the worse sense of the term, a pretender, one who acts a part, one who wears a mask to cover his true feelings, one who puts on an external show while inwardly his thoughts and feelings are very different.

To Jesus the scribes and Pharisees were people who were acting a part. What he meant was this. Their whole idea of religion consisted in outward observances, the wearing of elaborate phylacteries and tassels, the meticulous observance of the rules and regulations of the Law. But in their hearts there was bitterness and envy and pride and arrogance. To Jesus these scribes and Pharisees were persons who, under a mask of elaborate godliness, concealed hearts in which the most godless feelings and emotions held sway. And that accusation holds good in greater or lesser degree of anyone who lives life on the assumption that religion consists in external observances and external acts.

There is an unwritten saying of Jesus which says, "The key of the Kingdom they hid." His condemnation of these scribes and Pharisees is that they are not only failing to enter the Kingdom themselves, they shut the door on the faces of those who seek to enter. What did he mean by this accusation?

We have already seen (Matthew 6:10) that the best way to think of the Kingdom is to think of it as a society on earth where God's will is as perfectly done as it is in heaven. To be a citizen of the Kingdom, and to do God's will, are one and the same thing. The Pharisees believed that to do God's will was to observe their thousands of petty rules and regulations; and nothing could be further from that Kingdom whose basic idea is love. When people tried to find entry into the Kingdom the Pharisees presented them with these rules and regulations, which was as good as shutting the door in their faces.

The Pharisees preferred their ideas of religion to God's idea of religion. They had forgotten the basic truth that, one who would teach others must first listen to God. The gravest danger any teachers or preachers encounter is that they should erect their own prejudices into universal principles and substitute their own ideas for the truth of God. When they do that, they are not guides, but barriers to the Kingdom, for, misled themselves, they mislead others.

A strange feature of the ancient world was the repulsion and attraction which Judaism exercised over people at one and the same time. There was no more hated people than the Jews. Their separatism and their isolation and their contempt of other nations gained them hostility. It was, in fact, believed that a basic part of their religion was an oath that they would never under any circumstances give help to a Gentile, even to the extent of giving him directions if he asked the way. Their observance of the Sabbath gained them a reputation for laziness; their refusal of swine's flesh gained them mockery, even to the extent of the rumour that they worshipped the pig as their god. Anti-semitism was a real and universal force in the ancient world.

And yet there was an attraction. The idea of one God came as a wonderful thing to a world which believed in a multitude of gods. Jewish ethical purity and standards of morality had a fascination in a world steeped in immorality, especially for women. The result was that many were attracted to Judaism.

Their attraction was on two levels. There were those who were called the "God-fearers." These accepted the conception of one God; they accepted the Jewish moral law; but they took no part in the ceremonial law and did not become circumcised. Such people existed in large numbers, and were to be found listening and worshipping in every synagogue, and indeed provided Paul with his most fruitful field for evangelization. They are, for instance, the devout Greeks of Thessalonica (Acts 17:4).

It was the aim of the Pharisees to turn these God-fearers into *proselytes;* the word "proselyte" is an English transliteration of a Greek word *proselutos,* which means "one who has approached" or "drawn near." The proselyte was the full convert who had accepted the ceremonial law and circumcision and who had become in the fullest sense a Jew.

It was not to God the Pharisees sought to lead others; it was to their own sect of Pharisaism. That in fact was their sin. And is that sin even yet gone from the world, when it would still be insisted in certain quarters that a person must leave one church and become a member of another before being allowed a place at the Table of the Lord? The greatest of all heresies is the sinful conviction that any church has a monopoly of God or of his truth, or that any church is the only gateway to God's Kingdom.

Fourth Sunday in Lent

Luke 6:6–11

On another Sabbath Jesus went into the synagogue and was teaching, and there was a man there whose right hand was withered. The scribes and the Pharisees watched him to see if he would heal on the Sabbath day in order to find a charge against him. He knew well what they were thinking. He said to the man with the withered hand, "Rise, and stand in the midst." He rose and stood; Jesus said to them, "Here is a question for you—is it legal to do good on the Sabbath day or to do evil? To save a life or to destroy it?" He looked round on them and said to him, "Stretch out your hand." He did so and his hand was restored. They were filled with insane anger, and they discussed with each other what they could do to Jesus.

By this time the opposition to Jesus was quite open. He was teaching in the synagogue on the Sabbath day and the scribes and Pharisees were there with the set purpose of watching him so that, if he healed, they could charge him with breaking the Sabbath. There is this interesting touch. If we compare the story in Matthew 12:10–13 and

Mark 3:1–6 with Luke's version, we find that only Luke tells us that it was the man's right hand which was withered. There speaks the doctor, interested in the details of the case.

In this incident Jesus openly broke the law. To heal was to work and work was prohibited on the Sabbath day. True, if there was any danger to life, steps might be taken to help a sufferer. For instance, it was always legal to treat diseases of the eye or throat. But this man was in no danger of his life; he might have waited until the next day without peril. But Jesus laid down the great principle that, whatever the rules and regulations may say, it is always right to do a good thing on the Sabbath day. He asked the piercing questions, "Is it legal to save life or to destroy it on the Sabbath?" That must have struck home, for while he was seeking to help the life of the man, they were doing all they could to destroy him. It was he who was seeking to save and they who were seeking to destroy.

In this story there are three characters.

(i) There is the man with the withered hand. We can tell two things about him.

(a) One of the apocryphal gospels, that is, one which never gained admission into the New Testament, tells us that he was a stone mason and he came to Jesus, begging his help and saying, "I was a stone mason earning my living with my hand; I beseech you, Jesus, give me back my health that I may not have to beg my bread with shame." He was a man who wanted to work. God always looks with approval on the person who wants to do an honest day's work.

(b) He was a man who was prepared to attempt the impossible. He did not argue when Jesus told him to stretch out his useless hand; he tried and, in the strength Jesus gave him, he succeeded. Impossible is a word which should be banished from the vocabulary of the Christian. As a famous scientist said, "The difference between the difficult and the impossible is only that the impossible takes a little longer to do."

(ii) There is Jesus. There is in this story a glorious atmosphere of defiance. Jesus knew that he was being watched but without hesitation he healed. He bade the man stand out in the midst. This thing was not going to be done in a corner. There is a story of one of Wesley's preachers who proposed to preach in a hostile town. He hired the town-crier to announce the meeting and the town-crier announced it in a terrified whisper. The preacher took the bell from him and rang it and thundered out. "Mr So and So will preach in such and such a place and at such and such a time tonight—and I am the man." Real Christians display with pride the banner of their faith and bid the opposition do its worst.

(iii) There are the Pharisees. Here were leaders who took the quite extraordinary course of hating a person who had just cured a sufferer. They are the outstanding example of people who loved their rules and regulations more than they loved God. We see this happen in churches over and over again. Disputes are not about the great matters of the faith but about matters of church government and the like. Leighton once said, "The mode of church government is unconstrained; but peace and concord, kindness and goodwill are indispensable." There is an ever-present danger of setting loyalty to a system above loyalty to God.

23rd Day of Lent

Luke 20:45–47

While all the people were listening, Jesus said to his disciples, "Beware of the scribes who like to walk about in long robes, and who love greetings in the market places, and the chief seats in synagogues, and the top place at banquets. They devour widows' houses and pretend to offer long prayers. These will receive the greater condemnation."

The honours which the scribes and rabbis expected to receive were quite extraordinary. They had rules of precedence all carefully drawn up. In the college the most learned rabbi took precedence; at a banquet, the oldest. It is on record that two rabbis came in, after walking on the street, grieved and bewildered because more than one person had greeted them with, "May your peace be great," without adding, "My masters!" They claimed to rank even above parents. They said, "Let your esteem for your friend border on your esteem for your teacher, and let your respect for your teacher border on your reverence for God." "Respect for a teacher should exceed respect for a father, for both father and son owe respect to a teacher." "If a man's father and teacher have lost anything, the teacher's loss has the precedence, for a man's father only brought him into this world; his teacher, who taught him wisdom, brought him into the life of the world to come. . . . If a man's father and teacher are carrying burdens, he must first help his teacher, and afterwards his father. If his father and teacher are in captivity, he must first ransom his teacher, and afterwards his father." Such claims are almost incredible; it was not good for a person to make them; it was still less good to have them conceded. But it was claims like that the scribes and rabbis made.

Jesus also accused the scribes of devouring widows' houses. A rabbi was legally bound to teach for nothing. All rabbis were supposed to have trades and to support themselves by the work of their hands, while their teaching was given free. That sounds very noble but it was deliberately taught that to support a rabbi was an act of the greatest piety. "Whoever," they said, "puts part of his income into the purse of the wise is counted worthy of a seat in the heavenly academy." "Whosoever harbours a disciple of the wise in his house is counted as if he offered a daily sacrifice." "Let thy house be a place of resort to wise men." It is by no means extraordinary that impressionable women were the legitimate prey of the less scrupulous and more comfort-loving rabbis. At their worst, they did devour widows' houses.

The whole unhealthy business shocked and revolted Jesus. It was all the worse because these leaders knew so much better and held so responsible a place within the life of the community. God will always condemn those who use a position of trust to further their own ends and to pander to their own comfort.

24th Day of Lent

John 7:31–32, 45–52

Many of the crowd believed in him. "When the Anointed One of God comes," they said, "surely he cannot do greater signs than this man has done?" The Pharisees heard the crowds carrying on these discussions about him; and the chief priests and Pharisees despatched officers to arrest him. . . . So the officers came to the chief priests and the Pharisees. They said to them: "Why did you not bring him here?" The attendants answered: "Never did a man speak as he speaks." So the Pharisees answered: "Surely you too have not been led astray? Has anyone from the authorities believed in him? Or anyone from the Pharisees? They have not; but the mob which is ignorant of the law and which is accursed believes in him!" Nicodemus (the man who came to him before) said to them, for he was one of them: "Surely our law does not condemn a man unless it first hears a statement of the case from him, and has first-hand information about what he is doing?" They answered him: "Surely you too are not from Galilee? Search and see that no prophet arises from Galilee."

We have certain vivid reactions to Jesus.

(i) The reaction of the officers was bewildered amazement. They had gone out to arrest Jesus and had come back without him, because never in their lives had they heard anyone speak as he did. Really to listen to Jesus is an unparalleled experience for anyone.

(ii) The reaction of the chief priests and Pharisees was contempt. The Pharisees had a phrase by which they described the ordinary, simple people who did not observe the thousands of regulations of the ceremonial law. They called them "the People of the Land"; to them they were beneath contempt. To marry a daughter to one of them was like exposing her bound and helpless to a beast. "The masses who do not know the law are accursed." The rabbinic law said: "Six things are laid down about the People of the Land: entrust no testimony to them, take no testimony from them, trust them with no secret, do not appoint then guardians of an orphan, do not make them custodians of charitable funds, do not accompany them on a journey." It was forbidden to be a guest of one of the People of the Land, or to entertain such a person as a guest. It was even laid down that, wherever it was possible, nothing should be bought or sold from one of them. In their proud aristocracy and intellectual snobbery and spiritual pride, the Pharisees looked down in contempt on ordinary people. Their plea was: "Nobody who is spiritually and academically of any account has believed on Jesus. Only ignorant fools accept him." It is indeed a terrible thing when people think themselves either too clever or too good to need Jesus Christ—and it happens still.

(iii) There was the reaction of Nicodemus. It was a timid reaction, for he did not defend Jesus directly. He dared only to quote certain legal maxims which were relevant. The law laid it down that every person must receive justice (Exodus 23:1; Deuteronomy 1:16); and part of justice was and is to have the right to state one's own case and not be condemned on secondhand information. The Pharisees proposed to break that law, but it is clear that Nicodemus did not carry his protest any further. His heart told him to defend Jesus but his head told him not to take the risk. The Pharisees flung catchwords at him; they told him that obviously no prophet could come out of Galilee and taunted him with having a connection with the Galilaean rabble, and he said no more.

Often we find ourselves in situations in which we would like to defend Jesus and in which we know we ought to show our colours. Often we make a kind of half-hearted defence, and are then reduced to an uncomfortable and ashamed silence. In our defence of Jesus Christ it is better to be reckless with our hearts than prudent with our heads. To stand up for him may bring us mockery and unpopularity; it may even mean hardship and sacrifice. But the fact remains that Jesus said he would confess before his Father everyone who confessed him on earth, and deny before his Father anyone who denied him on earth. Loyalty to Christ may produce a cross on earth, but it brings a crown in eternity.

25th Day of Lent

Mark 2:15–17

Jesus was sitting at a meal in Levi's house, and many tax-collectors and sinners were sitting with Jesus and his disciples, for there were many of them, and they sought his company. When the experts in the law, who belonged to the school of the Pharisees, saw that he was eating in the company of sinners and tax-gatherers, they began to say to his disciples, "It is with tax-collectors and sinners that he is eating and drinking." Jesus

*heard them. "It is not those who are in good health who need a doctor,"
he said, "but those who are ill. I did not come to bring an invitation to
people who think that they have no faults but to those who know that they
are sinners."*

Once again Jesus is flinging down the gauntlet of defiance. When
Matthew had yielded himself to Jesus, he invited him to his house.
Naturally, having discovered Jesus for himself, he wished his friends
to share his great discovery—and his friends were like himself. It
could not be any other way. Matthew had chosen a job which cut
him off from the society of all respectable and orthodox people, and
he had to find his friends among outcasts like himself. Jesus gladly
accepted that invitation; and these outcasts of society sought his
company.

Nothing could better show the difference between Jesus and the
scribes and Pharisees and orthodox good people of the day. They were
not the kind of people whose company a sinner would have sought.
The sinner would have been looked at with bleak condemnation and
arrogant superiority and would have been frozen out of such company even before entering it.

By going to Matthew's house and sitting at his table and compa-
nying with his friends Jesus was defying the orthodox conventions of
his day.

We need not for a moment suppose that all these people were sinners in the moral sense of the term. The word "sinner" (*hamartolos*)
had a double significance. It did mean a person who broke the moral
law; but it also meant one who did not observe the scribal law. Those
who committed adultery and those who ate pork were both sinners;
persons who were guilty of theft and murder and persons who did not
wash their hands the required number of times and in the required
way before they ate were both sinners. These guests of Matthew no
doubt included many who had broken the moral law and played fast
and loose with life; but no doubt they also included many whose only
sin was that they did not observe the scribal rules and regulations.

When Jesus was taxed with this shocking conduct his answer was quite simple. "A doctor," he said "goes where he is needed. People in good health do not need him; sick people do; I am doing just the same; I am going to those who are sick in soul and who need me most."

Verse 17 is a highly concentrated verse. It sounds at first hearing as if Jesus had no use for good people. But the point of it is that the kind of persons for whom Jesus can do nothing are the ones who think themselves so good that they do not need anything done for them; and the ones for whom Jesus can do everything are the persons who are sinners and know it, who long in their hearts for a cure. To have no sense of need is to have erected a barrier between us and Jesus; to have a sense of need is to possess the passport to his presence.

The attitude of the orthodox Jews to the sinner was really compounded of two things.

(i) It was compounded of contempt. "The ignorant man," said the Rabbis, "can never be pious." Heraclitus, the Greek philosopher, was an arrogant aristocrat. One called Scythinus undertook to put his discourses into verse so that ordinary unlettered folk might read and understand them. The reaction of Heraclitus was put into an epigram. "Heraclitus am I. Why do ye drag me up and down, ye illiterate? It was not for you I toiled, but for such as understand me. One man in my sight is a match for thirty thousand, but the countless hosts do not make a single one." For the mob he had nothing but contempt. The scribes and Pharisees despised the common people; Jesus loved them. The scribes and Pharisees stood on their little eminence of formal piety and looked down on sinners; Jesus came and sat beside them, and by sitting beside them lifted them up.

(ii) It was compounded of fear. The orthodox were afraid of the contagion of the sinner; they were afraid that they might be infected with sin. They were like a doctor who would refuse to attend a case of infectious illness for fear of contracting it. Jesus was the one who forgot himself in a great desire to save others. C. T. Studd, great missionary of Christ, had four lines of doggerel that he loved to quote:

Some want to live within the sound
Of Church or Chapel bell;
I want to run a rescue shop
Within a yard of Hell.

The person whose heart is filled with contempt and fear can never take the gospel to others.

26th Day of Lent

John 8:12–20

So Jesus again continued to speak to them. "I am the Light of the World," he said. "He who follows me will not walk in darkness, but he will have the light of life." So the Pharisees said to him: "You are bearing witness about yourself. Your witness is not true." Jesus answered: "Even if I do bear witness about myself, my witness is true, because I know where I came from and where I am going to. You do not know where I came from and where I am going to. You form your judgments on purely human grounds. I do not judge anyone. But if I do form a judgment, my judgment is true, because I am not alone in my judgment, but I and the Father who sent me join in such a judgment. It stands written in your law, that the witness of two persons is to be accepted as true. It is I who witness about myself, and the Father who sent me also witnesses about me." They said to him: "Where is your Father?" Jesus answered: "You know neither me nor my Father. If you had known me you would know my Father too." He spoke these words in the treasury while he was teaching in the Temple precincts; and no one laid violent hands upon him, because his hour had not yet come.

In this passage Jesus makes the great claim: "I am the Light of the World." It is very likely that the background against which he made it made it doubly vivid and impressive. The festival with which John connects these discourses is the Festival of Tabernacles (John 7:2). We have already seen (John 7:37) how its ceremonies lent drama to Jesus' claim to give living water to all who would accept it. But there was another ceremony connected with this festival.

On the evening of its first day there was a ceremony called The Illumination of the Temple. It took place in the Court of the Women. The court was surrounded with deep galleries, erected to hold the spectators. In the centre four great candelabra were prepared. When the dark came the four great candelabra were lit and, it was said, they sent such a blaze of light throughout Jerusalem that every courtyard was lit up with their brilliance. Then all night long, until cock-crow the next morning, the greatest and the wisest and the holiest men in Israel danced before the Lord and sang psalms of joy and praise while the people watched. Jesus is saying in effect: "You have seen the blaze of the Temple illuminations piercing the darkness of the night. I am the Light of the World, and, for those who follow me there will be light, not only for one exciting night, but for all the pathways of life. The light in the Temple is a brilliant light, but in the end it flickers and dies. I am the Light which lasts for ever."

Jesus said: "He who follows me will not walk in darkness, but will have the light of life." "The light of life" means two things. The Greek can mean either the light which issues from the source of life or the light which gives life. In this passage it means both. Jesus is the very light of God come into the world; and he is the light which gives life to all persons. Just as the flower can never blossom when it never sees the sunlight, so our lives can never flower with the grace and beauty they ought to have until they are irradiated with the light of the presence of God in Jesus.

In this passage Jesus talks of "following" him. We often speak of following Jesus; we often urge people to do so. What do we mean? The Greek for "to follow" is *akolouthein;* and its meanings combine to shed a flood of light on what it means to follow Jesus. *Akolouthein* has five different but closely connected meanings.

(i) It is often used of a soldier following his captain.

(ii) It is often used of a slave accompanying his master.

(iii) It is often used of accepting a wise counsellor's opinion.

(iv) It is often used of giving obedience to the laws of a city or a state.

(v) It is often used of following a teacher's line of argument, or of following the gist of someone's speech. To be a follower of Christ is to give oneself, body, soul and spirit in obedience to the Master; and to enter upon that "following" is to walk in the light.

When we walk alone we are bound to stumble and grope, for so many of life's problems are beyond our solution. When we walk alone we are bound to take the wrong way, because we have no secure map of life. We need the heavenly wisdom to walk the earthly way. The one who has a sure guide and an accurate map is the one who is bound to come in safety to journey's end. Jesus Christ is that guide; he alone possesses the map to life. To follow him is to walk in safety through life and afterwards to enter into glory.

27th Day of Lent

Mark 11:27–33

Once again they came to Jerusalem, and, when Jesus was walking in the Temple, the chief priests and the experts in the law and the elders came to him, and said to him, "By what kind of authority do you do these things? Or, who gave you authority to do these things?" Jesus said, "I will put one point to you, and, if you answer me, I will tell you by what kind of authority I do these things. Was the baptism of John from heaven? or was it from men? Answer me!" They discussed the matter among themselves. "If," they said, "we say, 'From heaven,' he will say, 'Why did you not believe in it?' But, are we to say, 'From men?'"—for they were afraid of the people, for all truly held that John was a prophet. So they answered Jesus, "We do not know." So Jesus said to them, "Neither do I tell you by what kind of authority I do these things."

In the sacred precincts there were two famous cloisters, one on the east and one on the south side of the Court of the Gentiles. The one on the east was called Solomon's Porch. It was a magnificent arcade made by Corinthian columns 35 feet high. The one on the south was even more splendid. It was called the Royal Cloister. It was formed by four rows of white marble columns, each 6 feet in diameter and 30 feet high. There were 162 of them. It was common for rabbis and teachers to stroll among these columns and to teach as they walked. Most of the great cities of ancient times had these cloisters. They gave shelter from the sun and the wind and the rain, and, in point of fact, it was in these places that most of the religious and philosophic teaching was done. One of the most famous schools of ancient thought was that of the Stoics. They received their name from the fact that Zeno, their founder, taught as he walked in the *Stoa Poikile,* "the Painted Porch," in Athens. The word *stoa* means "porch" or "arcade" and the Stoics were the school of the porch. It was in these cloisters in the Temple that Jesus was walking and teaching.

To him there came a deputation of the chief priests and the experts in the law, that is the scribes, rabbis and elders. This was in reality a deputation from the Sanhedrin, of which these three groups formed the component parts. They asked a most natural question. For a private individual, all on his own, to clear the Court of the Gentiles of its accustomed and official traders was a staggering thing. So they asked Jesus, "By what kind of authority do you act like that?"

Jesus saw quite clearly the dilemma in which they sought to involve him, and his reply put them into a dilemma which was still worse. He said that he would answer on condition that they would answer one question for him, "Was John the Baptist's work, in your opinion, human or divine?"

This impaled them on the horns of a dilemma. If they said it was divine, they knew that Jesus would ask why they had stood out against it. Worse than that—if they said it was divine, Jesus could reply that John had in fact pointed everyone to him, and that therefore he was divinely attested and needed no further authority. If these members of the Sanhedrin agreed that John's work was divine, they would be compelled to accept Jesus as the Messiah. On the other hand, if they said that John's work was merely human, now that John had the added distinction of being a martyr, they knew quite well that the listening people would cause a riot. So they were compelled to say weakly that they did not know, and thereby Jesus escaped the need to give them any answer to their question.

The whole story is a vivid example of what happens to those who will not face the truth. They have to twist and wriggle and in the end get themselves into a position in which they are so helplessly involved that they have nothing to say. The ones who face the truth may have the humiliation of saying that they were wrong, or the peril of standing by it, but at least the future for them is strong and bright. The ones who will not face the truth have nothing but the prospect of deeper and deeper involvement in a situation which renders them helpless and ineffective.

28th Day of Lent

John 8:21–30

So he said to them again: "I am going away, and you will search for me, and you will die in your sin. You cannot come where I am going." So the Jews said: "Surely he is not going to kill himself, because he is saying: 'You cannot come where I am going'?" He said to them: "You are from below, but I am from above. You belong to this world, but I do not belong to this world. I said to you that you will die in your sins. For if you will not believe that I am who I am, you will die in your sins." They said to him: "Who are you?" Jesus said to them: "Anything I am saying to you is only the beginning. I have many things to say about you, and many judgments to deliver on you; but he who sent me is true, and I speak to the world what I have heard from him." They did not know that it was about the Father that he was speaking to them. So Jesus said to them: "When you lift up the Son of Man, then you will know that I am who I am, and that I do nothing on my own authority, but that I speak these things as the Father has taught me. And he who sent me is with me. He has not left me alone, because I always do the things that are pleasing to him." As he said these things, many believed in him.

Jesus begins by telling his opponents that he is going away; and that, after he is gone, they will realize what they have missed, and will search for him and not find him. This is the true prophetic note. It reminds us of three things. (i) There are certain opportunities which come and which do not return. To everyone is given the opportunity to accept Christ as Saviour and Lord; but that opportunity can be refused and lost. (ii) Implicit in this argument is the truth that life and time are limited. It is within an allotted span that we must make our decision for Christ. The time we have to make that decision is limited—and none of us knows what the limit is. There is therefore every reason for making it now. (iii) Just because there is opportunity in life there is also judgment. The greater the opportunity, the more clearly it beckons, the oftener it comes, the greater the judgment if it be refused or missed. This passage brings us face to face with the glory of our opportunity, and the limitation of time in which to seize it.

When Jesus spoke about going away, he was speaking about his return to his Father and to his glory. That was precisely where his opponents could not follow him, because by their continuous disobedience and their refusal to accept him, they had shut themselves off from God. His opponents met his words with a grim and mocking jest. Jesus said that they could not follow where he went; and they suggested that perhaps he was going to kill himself. The point is that, according to Jewish thought, the depths of hell were reserved for those who took their own lives. With a kind of grim blasphemy, they were saying: "Maybe he will take his own life; maybe he is on the way to the depths of Hell; it is true that we cannot and will not follow him there."

Jesus said that if they continued to refuse him they would die in their sins. That is a prophetic phrase (cp. Ezekiel 3:18; 18:18). There are two things involved there. (i) The word for sin is *hamartia,* which originally had to do with shooting and literally means "a missing of the target." Those who refuse to accept Jesus as Saviour and Lord have missed the target in life. They die with life unrealized, and therefore die unfitted to enter into the higher life with God. (ii) The essence of sin is that it separates people from God. When Adam, in the old story, committed the first sin, his first instinct was to hide himself from God (Genesis 3:8–10). The one who dies in sin dies at enmity with God; the one who accepts Christ already walks with God, and death only opens the way to a closer walk. To refuse Christ is to be a stranger to God; to accept him is to be the friend of God, and in that friendship the fear of death is forever banished.

Into this world which has gone wrong comes Christ; and Christ comes with the cure. He brings forgiveness; he brings cleansing; he brings strength and grace to live as humans ought and to make the world what it ought to be. But people can refuse a cure. A doctor may tell a patient that a certain treatment is able to restore health; may actually warn that without the treatment, death is inevitable. That is precisely what Jesus is saying: "If you will not believe that I am who I am you will die in your sins."

There is no verse in all the New Testament more difficult to translate than John 8:25. No one can really be sure what the Greek means. It could mean: "Even what I have told you from the beginning," which is the meaning the Revised Standard Version takes. Other suggested translations are: "Primarily, essentially, I am what I am telling you." "I declare to you that I am the beginning." "How is it that I even speak to you at all?" which is the translation of Moffatt. It is suggested in our translation that it may mean: "Everything I am saying to you now is only a beginning." If we take it like that, the passage goes on to say that people will see the real meaning of Christ in three ways.

(i) They will see it in the cross. It is when Christ is lifted up that we really see what he is. It is there we see the love that will never let us go and which loves us to the end.

(ii) They will see it in the Judgment. He has many judgments still to pass. At the moment he might look like the outlawed carpenter of Nazareth; but the day will come when all will see him as judge and know what he is.

(iii) When that happens they will see in him the embodied will of God. "I always do the things that are pleasing to him," Jesus said. Others, however good, are spasmodic in their obedience. The obedience of Jesus is continuous, perfect and complete. The day must come when everyone will see that in him is the very mind of God.

Fifth Sunday in Lent

Luke 20:19–26

The scribes and chief priests tried to lay hands on Jesus at that very hour; and they feared the people, for they realized that he spoke this parable to them. They watched for an opportunity, and they despatched spies, who

pretended that they were genuinely concerned about the right thing to do,
so that they might fasten on what he said and be able to hand him over
to the power and the authority of the governor. They asked him, "Teacher,
we know that you speak and teach rightly, and you are no respecter of per-
sons. Is it lawful for us to pay tribute to Caesar? Or not?" He saw their
subtle deception and said to them, "Show me a denarius. Whose image
and inscription is on it?" They said, "Caesar's." "Well then," he said to
them, "give to Caesar what belongs to Caesar, and give to God what be-
longs to God." There was nothing in this statement that they could fasten
on to in the presence of the people. They were amazed at his answer, and
had nothing to say.

Here the emissaries of the Sanhedrin returned to the attack. They sub-
orned men to go to Jesus and ask a question as if it was really trou-
bling their consciences. The tribute to be paid to Caesar was a poll-tax
of one *denarius,* about 4p, per year. Every man from 14 to 65 and
every woman from 12 to 65 had to pay that simply for the privilege
of existing. This tribute was a burning question in Palestine and had
been the cause of more than one rebellion. It was not the merely fi-
nancial question which was at stake. The tribute was not regarded as
a heavy imposition and was in fact no real burden at all. The issue at
stake was this—the fanatical Jews claimed that they had no king but
God and held that it was wrong to pay tribute to anyone other than
him. The question was a religious question, for which many were willing to die.

So, then, these emissaries of the Sanhedrin attempted to impale
Jesus on the horns of a dilemma. If he said that the tribute should not
be paid, they would at once report him to Pilate and arrest would follow as surely as the night the day. If he said that it should be paid, he
would alienate many of his supporters, especially the Galilaeans,
whose support was so strong.

Jesus answered them on their own grounds. He asked to be shown
a *denarius.* Now, in the ancient world the sign of kingship was the issue of currency. For instance, the Maccabees had immediately issued
their own currency whenever Jerusalem was freed from the Syrians.

Further, it was universally admitted that to have the right to issue currency carried with it the right to impose taxation. A ruler had the right to put the royal image and superscription on a coin, and *ipso facto* had the right to impose taxation. So Jesus said, "If you accept Caesar's currency and use it, you are bound to accept Caesar's right to impose taxes"; "but," he went on, "there is a domain in which Caesar's writ does not run and which belongs wholly to God."

(i) Those who live in a state and enjoy all its privileges cannot divorce themselves from it. The more honest people are, the better citizens they will be. There should be no better and no more conscientious citizens of any state than its Christians; and one of the tragedies of modern life is that Christians do not sufficiently take their part in the government of the state. If they abandon their responsibilities and leave materialistic politicians to govern, Christians cannot justifiably complain about what is done or not done.

(ii) Nonetheless, it remains true that in the life of the Christian God has the last word and not the state. The voice of conscience is louder than the voice of any human laws. Christians are at once the servants and the conscience of the state. Just because they are the best of citizens, they will refuse to do what Christian citizens cannot do. They will at one and the same time fear God and honour the king.

29th Day of Lent

Matthew 22:1–10

Jesus again answered them in parables: "The Kingdom of Heaven is like the situation which arose when a man who was a king arranged a wedding for his son. He sent his servants to summon those who had been invited to the wedding, and they refused to come. He again sent other servants. 'Tell those who have been invited,' he said, 'look you, I have my meal all prepared; my oxen and my specially fattened animals have been killed; and everything is ready. Come to the wedding.' But they disregarded the invitation and went away, one to his estate, and another to his business. The rest seized the servants and treated them shamefully and killed them. The king was angry, and sent his armies, and destroyed those murderers, and set fire to their city. Then he said to his servants, 'The wedding is ready. Those who have been invited did not deserve to come. Go, then, to the highways and invite to the wedding all you may find.' So the servants went out to the roads, and collected all whom they found, both bad and good; and the wedding was supplied with guests."

Verses 1–14 of this chapter form not one parable, but two; and we will grasp their meaning far more easily and far more fully if we take them separately.

The events of the first of the two were completely in accordance with normal Jewish customs. When the invitations to a great feast, like a wedding feast, were sent out, the time was not stated; and when everything was ready the servants were sent out with a final summons to tell the guests to come. So, then, the king in this parable had long ago sent out his invitations; but it was not till everything was prepared that the final summons was issued—and insultingly refused. This parable has two meanings.

(i) It has a purely local meaning. Its local meaning was a driving home of what had already been said in the Parable of the Wicked Husbandmen; once again it was an accusation of the Jews. The invited guests who when the time came refused to come, stand for the Jews. Ages ago they had been invited by God to be his chosen people; yet when God's son came into the world, and they were invited to follow him they contemptuously refused. The result was that the invitation of God went out direct to the highways and the byways; and the people in the highways and the byways stand for the sinners and the Gentiles, who never expected an invitation into the Kingdom.

As the writer of the Gospel saw it, the consequences of the refusal were terrible. There is one verse of the parable which is strangely out of place; and that because it is not part of the original parable as Jesus told it, but an interpretation by the writer of the Gospel. That is verse 7, which tells how the king sent his armies against those who refused the invitation, and burned their city.

This introduction of armies and the burning of the city seems at first sight completely out of place taken in connexion with invitations to a wedding feast. But Matthew was composing his Gospel some time between A.D. 80 and 90. What had happened during the period between the actual life of Jesus and now? The answer is—the destruction of Jerusalem by the armies of Rome in A.D. 70. The Temple was sacked and burned and the city destroyed stone from stone, so that a plough was drawn across it. Complete disaster had come to those who refused to recognize the Son of God when he came.

(ii) Equally this parable has much to say on a much wider scale.

(a) It reminds us that the invitation of God is to a feast as joyous as a wedding feast. His invitation is to joy. To think of Christianity as a gloomy giving up of everything which brings laughter and sunshine and happy fellowship is to mistake its whole nature. It is to joy that Christians are invited; and it is joy they miss, if they refuse the invitation.

(b) It reminds us that the things which make people deaf to the invitation of Christ are not necessarily bad in themselves. One went to his estate; the other to his business. They did not go off on a wild carousal or an immoral adventure. They went off on the, in itself, excellent task of efficiently administering their business life. It is very easy for us to be so busy with the things of time that we forget the things of eternity, to be so preoccupied with the things which are seen that we forget the things which are unseen, to hear so insistently the claims of the world that we cannot hear the soft invitation of the voice of Christ. The tragedy of life is that it is so often the second bests which shut out the bests, that it is things which are good in themselves which shut out the things that are supreme. We can be so busy making a living that we fail to make a life; we can be so busy with the administration and the organization of life that we forget life itself.

(c) It reminds us that the appeal of Christ is not so much to consider how we will be punished as it is to see what we will miss, if we do not take his way of things. Those who would not come were punished, but their real tragedy was that they lost the joy of the wedding feast. If we refuse the invitation of Christ, some day our greatest pain will lie, not in the things we suffer, but in the realization of the precious things we have missed.

(d) It reminds us that in the last analysis God's invitation is the invitation of grace. Those who were gathered in from the highways and the byways had no claim on the king at all; they could never by any stretch of imagination have expected an invitation to the wedding feast, still less could they ever have deserved it. It came to them from nothing other than the wide-armed, open-hearted, generous hospitality of the king. It was grace which offered the invitation and grace which gathered people in.

30th Day of Lent

John 11:47–53

The chief priests and Pharisees assembled the Sanhedrin: "What are we going to do?" they said, "because this man does many signs. If we leave him alone like this, all will believe in him, and the Romans will come and will take away our place and will destroy our nation." One of them, called Caiaphas, who was High Priest for that year, said to them: "You are witless creatures. You do not think it out that it is to our good that one man should die for the people, rather than that the whole nation should perish." It was not he who was responsible for what he said; but, since he was High Priest for that year, he was really prophesying that Jesus was going to die for the nation, and, not only for the nation, but that the scattered children of God should be gathered into one. So from that day they plotted to kill him.

The Jewish authorities are very vividly sketched before us. The wonderful happening at Bethany had forced their hand; it was impossible to allow Jesus to continue unchecked, otherwise the people would follow him in ever larger numbers. So the Sanhedrin was called to deal with the situation.

In the Sanhedrin there were both Pharisees and Sadducees. The Pharisees were not a political party at all; their sole interest was in living according to every detail of the law; and they cared not who governed them so long as they were allowed to continue in meticulous obedience to the law. On the other hand, the Sadducees were intensely political. They were the wealthy and aristocratic party. They were also the collaborationist party. So long as they were allowed to retain their wealth, comfort and position of authority, they were well content to collaborate with Rome. All the priests were Sadducees. And it is clear that it was the priests who dominated this meeting of the Sanhedrin. That is to say, it was the Sadducees who did all the talking.

With a few masterly strokes John delineates their characteristics. First, they were notoriously discourteous. Josephus said of them (*The Wars of the Jews* 2:8, 14) that: "The behaviour of the Sadducees to one another is rather rude, and their intercourse with their equals is rough, as with strangers." "You know nothing at all," said Caiaphas (verse 49). "You are witless, brainless creatures." Here we see the innate, domineering arrogance of the Sadducees in action; this was exactly in character. Their contemptuous arrogance is an implicit contrast to the accents of love of Jesus.

Second, the one thing at which the Sadducees always aimed was the retention of their political and social power and prestige. What they feared was that Jesus might gain a following and raise a disturbance against the government. Now, Rome was essentially tolerant, but, with such a vast empire to govern, it could never afford civil disorder, and always quelled it with a firm and merciless hand. If Jesus was the cause of civil disorder, Rome would descend in all her power, and, beyond a doubt the Sadducees would be dismissed from their positions of authority. It never even occurred to them to ask whether Jesus was right or wrong. Their only question was: "What effect will this have on our ease and comfort and authority?" They judged things, not in the light of principle but in the light of their own career. And it is still possible for persons to set their own careers before the will of God.

Then comes the first tremendous example of dramatic irony. Sometimes in a play a character says something without realizing its full significance; that is dramatic irony. So the Sadducees insisted that Jesus must be eliminated or the Romans would come and take their authority away. In A.D. 70 that is exactly what happened. The Romans, weary of Jewish stubbornness, besieged Jerusalem, and left it a heap of ruins with a plough drawn across the Temple area. How different things might have been if the Jews had accepted Jesus! The very steps they took to save their nation destroyed it. This destruction happened in A.D. 70; John's Gospel was written about A.D. 100;

and all who read it would see the dramatic irony in the words of the Sadducees.

Then Caiaphas, the High Priest, made his two-edged statement. "If you had any sense," he said, "you would come to the conclusion that it is far better that one person should perish for the nation than that the whole nation should perish." It was the Jewish belief that when the High Priest asked God's counsel for the nation, God spoke through him. In the old story Moses chose Joshua to be his successor in the leadership of Israel. Joshua was to have a share in his honour and when he wished for God's counsel he was to go to Eleazar the High Priest: "And he shall stand before Eleazar the priest, who shall inquire for him . . . at his word they shall go out, and at his word they shall come in" (Numbers 27:18–21). The High Priest was to be the channel of God's word to the leader and to the nation. That is what Caiaphas was that day.

Here is another tremendous example of dramatic irony. Caiaphas meant that it was better that Jesus should die than that there should be trouble with the Romans. It was true that Jesus must die to save the nation. That was true—but not in the way that Caiaphas meant. It was true in a far greater and more wonderful way. God can speak through the most unlikely people, sometimes sending a message through someone without their ever being aware of it. God can use even the words of bad people.

31st Day of Lent

Matthew 23:37–39

"Jerusalem, Jerusalem, killer of the prophets, stoner of those sent to you, how often have I wished to gather your children together, as a bird gathers her nestlings under her wings—and you refused. Look you, your house is left to you desolate, for I tell you from now you will not see me until you will say, 'Blessed in the name of the Lord is he that comes.'"

Here is all the poignant tragedy of rejected love. Here Jesus speaks, not so much as the stern judge of all the earth, but as the lover of the souls of all people.

There is one curious light this passage throws on the life of Jesus which we may note in the passing. According to the Synoptic Gospels Jesus was never in Jerusalem after his public ministry began, until he came to this last Passover Feast. We can see here how much the Gospel story leaves out, for Jesus could not have said what he says here unless he had paid repeated visits to Jerusalem and issued to the people repeated appeals. A passage like this shows us that in the Gospels we have the merest sketch and outline of the life of Jesus.

This passage shows us four great truths.

(i) It shows us the patience of God. Jerusalem had killed the prophets and stoned the messengers of God; yet God did not cast her off; and in the end he sent his Son. There is a limitless patience in the love of God which bears with people's sinning and will not cast them off.

(ii) It shows us the appeal of Jesus. Jesus speaks as the lover. He will not force an entry; the only weapon he can use is the appeal of love. He stands with outstretched hands of appeal, an appeal which each person has the awful responsibility of being able to accept or to refuse.

(iii) It shows us deliberate sin. People looked on Christ in all the splendour of his appeal—and refused him. There is no handle on the outside of the door of the human heart; it must be opened from the inside; and sin is the open-eyed deliberate refusal of the appeal of God in Jesus Christ.

(iv) It shows us the consequences of rejecting Christ. Only forty years were to pass and in A.D. 70 Jerusalem would be a heap of ruins. That disaster was the direct consequence of the rejection of Jesus Christ. Had the Jews accepted the Christian way of love and abandoned the way of power politics, Rome would never have descended on them with its avenging might. It is the fact of history—even in time—that the nation which rejects God is doomed to disaster.

32nd Day of Lent

Matthew 25:31–46

"When the Son of Man shall come in his glory, and all the angels with him, then he will take his seat upon the throne of his glory, and all na-

tions will be assembled before him, and he will separate them from each
other, as a shepherd separates the sheep from the goats, and he will place
the sheep on his right hand and the goats on his left. Then the King will
say to those on his right hand, 'Come, you who are blessed by my Father,
enter into possession of the Kingdom which has been prepared for you since
the creation of the world. For I was hungry, and you gave me to eat; I was
thirsty, and you gave me to drink; I was a stranger, and you gathered me
in; naked, and you clothed me; I was sick, and you came to visit me; in
prison, and you came to me.' Then the righteous will answer him, 'Lord,
when did we see you hungry, and nourish you? Or thirsty, and gave you
to drink? When did we see you a stranger, and gather you to us? Or naked,
and clothed you? When did we see you sick, or in prison, and come to you?'
And the King will answer them, 'This is the truth I tell you—insomuch
as you did it to one of the least of these my brothers, you did it to me.'
Then he will say to those on the left, 'Go from me, you cursed ones, to the
eternal fire prepared for the devil and his angels. For I was hungry, and
you did not give me to eat; I was thirsty, and you did not give me to drink;
I was a stranger, and you did not gather me to you; naked, and you did
not clothe me; sick and in prison, and you did not come to visit me.' Then
these too will answer, 'Lord, when did we see you hungry, or thirsty, or a
stranger, or naked, or sick, or in prison, and did not render service to you?'
Then he will answer them, 'This is the truth I tell you—in so far as you
did not do it to one of the least of these, you did not do it to me.' And these
will go away to eternal punishment, but the righteous will go away to
eternal life."

This is one of the most vivid parables Jesus ever spoke, and the lesson
is crystal clear—that God will judge us in accordance with our reaction to human need. His judgment does not depend on the knowledge we have amassed, or the fame that we have acquired, or the
fortune that we have gained, but on the help that we have given. And
there are certain things which this parable teaches us about the help
which we must give.

(i) It must be help in simple things. The things which Jesus picks
out—giving a hungry person a meal, or a thirsty one a drink, welcoming

a stranger, cheering the sick, visiting the prisoner—are things which anyone can do. It is not a question of giving away thousands of pounds, or of writing our names in the annals of history; it is a case of giving simple help to the people we meet every day. There never was a parable which so opened the way to glory to the simplest people.

(ii) It must be help which is uncalculating. Those who helped did not think that they were helping Christ and thus piling up eternal merit; they helped because they could not stop themselves. It was the natural, instinctive, quite uncalculating reaction of the loving heart. Whereas, on the other hand, the attitude of those who failed to help was, "If we had known it was you we would gladly have helped; but we thought it was only some common person who was not worth helping." It is still true that there are those who will help if they are given praise and thanks and publicity; but to help like that is not to help, it is to pander to self-esteem. Such help is not generosity; it is disguised selfishness. The help which wins the approval of God is that which is given for nothing but the sake of helping.

(iii) Jesus confronts us with the wonderful truth that all such help given is given to himself, and all such help withheld is withheld from himself. How can that be? If we really wish to delight a child's parents, if we really wish to move them to gratitude, the best way to do it is to help their child. God is the great Father; and the way to delight the heart of God is to help his children when we have the opportunity.

There were two persons who found this parable blessedly true. The one was Francis of Asissi. He was wealthy and high-born and high-spirited. But he was not happy. He felt that life was incomplete. Then one day he was out riding and met a leper, loathsome and repulsive in the ugliness of his disease. Something moved Francis to dismount and fling his arms around this wretched sufferer; and in his arms the face of the leper changed to the face of Christ.

The other was Martin of Tours. He was a Roman soldier and a Christian. One cold winter day, as he was entering a city, a beggar stopped him and asked for alms. Martin had no money; but the beggar was blue and shivering with cold, and Martin gave what he had.

He took off his soldier's coat, worn and frayed as it was; he cut it in two and gave half of it to the beggar. That night he had a dream. In it he saw the heavenly places and all the angels and Jesus in the midst of them; and Jesus was wearing half of a Roman soldier's cloak. One of the angels said to him, "Master, why are you wearing that battered old cloak? Who gave it to you?" And Jesus answered softly, "My servant Martin gave it to me."

When we learn the generosity which without calculation helps others in the simplest things, we too will know the joy of helping Jesus Christ himself.

33rd Day of Lent

John 3:14, 15
And as Moses lifted up the serpent in the wilderness, so the Son of Man must be lifted up, that every one who believes in him may have eternal life.

John goes back to a strange Old Testament story which is told in Numbers 21:4–9. On their journey through the wilderness the people of Israel murmured and complained and regretted that they had ever left Egypt. To punish them God sent a plague of deadly, fiery serpents; the people repented and cried for mercy. God instructed Moses to make an image of a serpent and to hold it up in the midst of the camp; and those who looked upon the serpent were healed. That story much impressed the Israelites. They told how in later times that brazen serpent became an idol and in the days of Hezekiah had to be destroyed because people were worshipping it (2 Kings 18:4). The Jews themselves were always a little puzzled by this incident in view of the fact that they were absolutely forbidden to make graven images. The rabbis explained it this way: "It was not the serpent that gave life. So long as Moses lifted up the serpent, they believed on him who had commanded Moses to act thus. It was God who healed them." The healing power lay not in the brazen serpent; it was only a symbol to turn their thoughts to God; and when they did that they were healed.

John took that old story and used it as a kind of parable of Jesus.

He says: "The serpent was lifted up; people looked at it; their thoughts were turned to God; and by the power of that God in whom they trusted they were healed. Even so Jesus must be lifted up; and when people turn their thoughts to him, and believe in him, they too will find eternal life."

In this passage we have two expressions whose meaning we must face. It will not be possible to extract all their meaning, because they both mean more than ever we can discover; but we must try to grasp at least something of it.

(i) There is the phrase which speaks of "believing in Jesus." It means at least three things.

(a) It means believing with all our hearts that God is as Jesus declared him to be. It means believing that God loves us, that God cares for us, that God wants nothing more than to forgive us.

(b) How can we be sure that Jesus knew what he was talking about? What guarantee is there that his wonderful good news is true? Here we come upon the second article in belief. We must believe that Jesus is the Son of God, that in him is the mind of God, that he knew God so well, was so close to God, was so one with God, that he could tell us the absolute truth about God.

(c) But belief has a third element. We believe that God is a loving Father because we believe that Jesus is the Son of God and that therefore what he says about God is true. Then comes this third element. We must stake everything on the fact that what Jesus says is true. Whatever he says we must do; whenever he commands we must obey. When he tells us to cast ourselves unreservedly on the mercy of God we must do so. We must take Jesus at his word. Every smallest action in life must be done in unquestioning obedience to him.

So then belief in Jesus has these three elements—belief that God is our loving Father, belief that Jesus is the son of God and therefore tells us the truth about God and life, and unswerving and unquestioning obedience to Jesus.

(ii) The second great phrase is "eternal life." We have already seen that eternal life is the very life of God himself. But let us ask this: if we possess eternal life, what do we have? If we enter into eternal life, what is it like? To have eternal life envelops every relationship in life with peace.

(a) It gives us peace with God. We are no longer cringing before a tyrannical king or seeking to hide from an austere judge. We are at home with our Father.

(b) It gives us peace with others. If we have been forgiven we must be forgiving. It enables us to see people as God sees them. It makes us and all humankind into one great family joined in love.

(c) It gives us peace with life. If God is Father, God is working all things together for good. Lessing used to say that if he had one question to ask the Sphinx, who knew everything, it would be: "Is this a friendly universe?" When we believe that God is Father, we also believe that such a father's hand will never cause his child a needless tear. We may not understand life any better, but we will not resent life any longer.

(d) It gives us peace with ourselves. In the last analysis people are more afraid of themselves than of anything else. We know our own weaknesses; we know the force of our own temptations; we know our own tasks and the demands of our own lives. But now we know that we are facing it all with God. It is not we who live but Christ who lives in us. There is a peace founded on strength in our lives.

(e) It makes us certain that the deepest peace on earth is only a shadow of the ultimate peace which is to come. It gives us a hope and a goal to which we travel. It gives us a life of glorious wonder here and yet, at the same time, a life in which the best is yet to be.

34th Day of Lent

John 12:1–8

Now six days before the Passover Jesus went to Bethany, where Lazarus was whom he raised from the dead. So they made him a meal there, and Martha was serving while Lazarus was one of those who reclined at table with him. Now Mary took a pound of very precious genuine spikenard ointment, and anointed Jesus' feet, and wiped his feet with her hair; and the house was filled with the perfume of the ointment. But Judas Iscariot, one of his disciples, the one who was going to betray him, said: "Why was

this ointment not sold for ten pounds, and the proceeds given to the poor?"
He said this, not that he cared for the poor, but because he was a thief
and had charge of the money-box, and pilfered from what was put into
it. So Jesus said: "Let her observe it now against the day of my burial. The
poor you have always with you, but me you have not always."

When Jesus came to Bethany they made him a meal. It must have
been in the house of Martha and Mary and Lazarus, for where else
would Martha be serving but in her own house? It was then that
Mary's heart ran over in love. She had a pound of very precious spikenard ointment. . . . With this perfume Mary anointed Jesus' feet. Judas ungraciously questioned her action as sheer waste. Jesus silenced
him by saying that money could be given to the poor at any time, but
a kindness done to him must be done now, for soon the chance would
be gone forever.

There is a whole series of little character sketches here.

(i) There is the character of Martha. She was serving at table. She
loved Jesus; she was a practical woman; and the only way in which she
could show her love was by the work of her hands. Martha always gave
what she could. Many and many great persons have been what they
were only because of someone else's loving care for their creature comforts. It is just as possible to serve Jesus in the kitchen as on the public platform or in a career lived in the eyes of the world.

(ii) There is the character of Mary. Mary was the one who above
all loved Jesus; and here in her action we see three things about love.

(a) We see love's extravagance. Mary took the most precious thing
she possessed and spent it all on Jesus. Love is not love if it nicely cal-
culates the cost. It gives its all and its only regret is that it has not still
more to give. . . .

(b) We see love's humility. It was a sign of honour to anoint a person's head. "Thou anointest my head with oil," says the psalmist
(Psalm 23:5). But Mary would not look so high as the head of Jesus;
she anointed his feet. The last thing Mary thought of was to confer
an honour upon Jesus; she never dreamed she was good enough for
that.

(c) We see love's unself-consciousness. Mary wiped Jesus' feet with the hair of her head. In Palestine no respectable woman would ever appear in public with her hair unbound. On the day a girl was married her hair was bound up, and never again would she be seen in public with her long tresses flowing loose. That was the sign of an immoral woman. But Mary never even thought of that. When two people really love each other they live in a world of their own. They will wander slowly down a crowded street hand in hand heedless of what other people think. Many are self-conscious about showing their Christianity, concerned always about what others are thinking about them. Mary loved Jesus so much that it was nothing to her what others thought.

(iii) There is the character of Judas. There are three things here about him.

(a) We see Jesus' trust in Judas. As far back as John 6:70, 71, John shows us Jesus well aware that there was a traitor within the ranks. It may well be that he tried to touch Judas's heart by making him the treasurer of the apostolic company. It may well be that he tried to appeal to his sense of honour. It may well be that he was saying in effect to him: "Judas, here's something that you can do for me. Here is proof that I need you and want you." That appeal failed with Judas, but the fact remains that often the best way to reclaim someone who is on the wrong path is to treat him not with suspicion but with trust; not as if we expected the worst, but as if we expected the best.

(b) We see one of the laws of temptation. Jesus would not have put Judas in charge of the money-box unless he had some capabilities in that direction. Westcott in his commentary said: "Temptation commonly comes through that for which we are naturally fitted." If a person is fitted to handle money, the temptation may be to regard money as the most important thing in the world. If one is fitted to occupy a place of prominence, the temptation may be to think first and foremost of reputation. If others have particular gifts, their temptation may be to become conceited about their own gifts. Judas had a gift for handling money and became so fond of it that he became first a thief and then a traitor for its sake. . . . Temptation struck him at the point of his special gift.

(c) We see how anyone's view can be warped. Judas had just seen an action of surpassing loveliness; and he called it extravagant waste. He was an embittered man and he took an embittered view of things. A person's sight depends on what is inside. We see only what we are fit and able to see. If we like others, they can do little wrong. If we dislike them, we may misinterpret their finest actions. A warped mind brings a warped view of things; and, if we find ourselves becoming very critical of others and imputing unworthy motives to them, we should, for a moment, stop examining them and start examining ourselves.

Lastly, there is here one great truth about life. Some things we can do almost any time, but some things we will never do, unless we grasp the chance when it comes. We are seized with the desire to do something fine and generous and big-hearted. But we put it off—we will do it tomorrow; and the fine impulse goes, and the thing is never done. Life is an uncertain thing. We think to utter some word of thanks or praise or love but we put it off; and often the word is never spoken.

Sixth Sunday in Lent: Palm Sunday, the Beginning of the Passion

Mark 11:7–10

They brought the colt to Jesus, and they put their garments on it, and mounted him on it. Many of them spread their garments on the road. Others cut branches from the fields and spread them on the road. And those who were going before and those who were following kept shouting, "Save now! Blessed is the coming kingdom of our father David! Send thy salvation from the heights of heaven!"

The colt they brought had never been ridden upon. That was fitting, for a beast to be used for a sacred purpose must never have been used for any other purpose. It was so with the red heifer whose ashes cleansed from pollution (Numbers 19:2; Deuteronomy 21:3).

The whole picture is of a populace who misunderstood. It shows us a crowd of people thinking of kingship in the terms of conquest in which they had thought of it for so long. It is oddly reminiscent of how Simon Maccabaeus entered Jerusalem a hundred and fifty years before, after he had blasted Israel's enemies in battle. "And he entered into it the three and twentieth day of the seventh month, in the hundred, seventy and first year, with thanksgiving and branches of palm trees, and with harps, and cymbals, and viols, and hymns and songs, because there was destroyed a great enemy out of Israel" (1 Maccabees 13:51). It was a conqueror's welcome they sought to give to Jesus, but they never dreamed of the kind of conqueror he wished to be.

The very shouts which the crowd raised to Jesus showed how their thoughts were running. When they spread their garments on the ground before him, they did exactly what the crowd did when that man of blood Jehu was anointed king (2 Kings 9:13). They shouted, "Blessed is he who comes in the name of the Lord!" That is a quotation from Psalm 118:26, and should really read a little differently, "Blessed in the name of the Lord is he who comes!"

There are three things to note about that shout.

  (i) It was the regular greeting with which pilgrims were addressed when they reached the Temple on the occasion of the great feasts.

  (ii) "He who comes" was another name for the Messiah. When the Jews spoke about the Messiah, they talked of him as the One who is Coming.

  (iii) But it is the whole origin of the Psalm from which the words come that makes them supremely suggestive. In 167 B.C. there had arisen an extraordinary king in Syria called Antiocheius. He had conceived it his duty to be a missionary of Hellenism and to introduce Greek ways of life, Greek thought and Greek religion wherever he could, even, if necessary, by force. He tried to do so in Palestine.

For a time he conquered Palestine. To possess a copy of the law or to circumcise a child were crimes punishable by death. He desecrated the Temple courts. He actually instituted the worship of Zeus where Jehovah had been worshipped. With deliberate insult he offered swine's flesh on the great altar of the burnt-offering. He made the chambers round the Temple courts into brothels. He did everything he could to wipe out the Jewish faith.

It was then that Judas Maccabaeus arose, and after an amazing career of conquest, in 163 B.C. he drove Antiocheius out and re-purified and re-consecrated the Temple, an event which the Feast of the Dedication, or the Feast of Hanukah, still commemorates. And in all probability Psalm 118 was written to commemorate that great day of purification and the battle which Judas Maccabaeus won. It is a conqueror's psalm.

Again and again we see the same thing happening in this incident. Jesus had claimed to be the Messiah, but in such a way as to try to show that the popular ideas of the Messiah were misguided. But the people did not see it. Their welcome was one which befitted, not the King of love, but the conqueror who would shatter the enemies of Israel.

In verses 9 and 10 there is the word *Hosanna.* The word is consistently misunderstood. It is quoted and used as if it meant "Praise"; but it is a simple transliteration of the Hebrew for "Save now!" It occurs in exactly the same form in 2 Samuel 14:4 and 2 Kings 6:26, where it is used by people seeking for help and protection at the hands of the king. When the people shouted *Hosanna* it was not a cry of praise to Jesus, which it often sounds like when we quote it. It was a cry to God to break in and save his people now that the Messiah had come.

No incident so shows the sheer courage of Jesus as this does. In the circumstances one might have expected him to enter Jerusalem secretly and to keep hidden from the authorities who were out to destroy him. Instead he entered in such a way that the attention of every eye was focussed upon him. One of the most dangerous things a person can do is to go to people and tell them that all their accepted ideas are wrong. Anyone who tries to tear up by the roots a people's nationalistic dreams is in for trouble. But that is what Jesus deliberately was doing. Here we see Jesus making the last appeal of love and making it with a courage that is heroic.

35th Day: Monday of Holy Week

John 12:20–22

There were some Greeks among those whose practice it was to come up to the feast. Now these came to Philip, who came from Bethsaida in Galilee, and made a request to him. "Sir," they said, "we wish to see Jesus." Philip went and told Andrew, and Andrew and Philip went and told Jesus.

How had these Greeks come to hear of Jesus and to be interested in him? J. H. Bernard throws out a most interesting suggestion. It was in the last week of his ministry that Jesus cleansed the Temple and swept the money-changers and the sellers of doves from the Temple court. Now these traders had their stance in the Court of the Gentiles, that great court which was the first of the Temple courts and where Gentiles were allowed to come but no further. If these Greeks were in Jerusalem at all they would be certain to visit the Temple and to stand in the Court of the Gentiles. Perhaps they had actually witnessed that tremendous scene when Jesus had driven the traders from the Temple court; and perhaps they wished to know more of one who could do things like that. However that may be, this is one of the great moments of the story, for here is the first faint hint of a gospel which is to go out to all the world.

John 12:23–26

Jesus answered them: "The hour has come that the Son of Man should be glorified. This is the truth I tell you—unless a grain of wheat falls into the ground and dies, it remains all by itself alone; but, if it dies, it bears much fruit. He who loves his life is losing it; and he who hates his life in this world will keep it to life eternal. If anyone will serve me, let him follow me; and where I am, there will my servants also be."

The first sentence which Jesus spoke would excite the hearts of those who heard it; then began a succession of sayings which must have left them staggered and bewildered by their sheer incredibility, for they spoke, not in terms of conquest, but in terms of sacrifice and death. We will never understand Jesus nor the attitude of the Jews to him, until we understand how he turned their ideas upside down, replacing a dream of conquest with a vision of a cross. No wonder they did not understand him; the tragedy is that they refused to try.

What was this amazing paradox which Jesus was teaching? He was saying three things, which are all variations of one central truth and all at the heart of the Christian faith and life.

(i) He was saying that only by death comes life. The grain of wheat was ineffective and unfruitful so long as it was preserved, as it were, in safety and security. It was when it was thrown into the cold ground, and buried there as if in a tomb, that it bore fruit. It was by the death of the martyrs that the church grew. In the famous phrase: "The blood of the martyrs was the seed of the church."

(ii) Jesus was saying that only by spending life do we retain it. Those who love their own life are moved by two aims, by selfishness and by the desire for security. Not once or twice but many times Jesus insisted that those who hoarded their own lives must in the end lose them, and the ones who spent their lives must in the end gain them. There was a famous evangelist called Christmas Evans who was always on the move preaching for Christ. His friends besought him to take things easier but his answer always was: "It is better to burn out than to rust out." When Joan of Arc knew that her enemies were strong and her time was short, she prayed to God: "I shall only last a year, use me as you can." Again and again Jesus laid down this law (Mark 8:35; Matthew 16:25; Luke 9:24; Matthew 10:39; Luke 17:33).

We have only to think of what this world would have lost if there had not been persons prepared to forget their personal safety, security, selfish gain and selfish advancement. The world owes everything to people who recklessly spent their strength and gave themselves to God and to others. No doubt we will exist longer if we take things easily, if we avoid all strain, if we sit at the fire and husband life, if we look after ourselves as a hypochondriac looks after his health. No doubt we will exist longer—but we will never live.

(iii) Jesus was saying that only by service comes greatness. The people whom the world remembers with love are the people who serve others. A certain Mrs. Berwick had been very active in Salvation Army work in Liverpool. She retired to London. There came the war and the air raids. People get queer ideas and the idea got about that somehow Mrs. Berwick's poor house and her shelter were specially safe. She was old now; her Liverpool days of social service were long behind her; but she felt she must do something about it. So she got together a simple first-aid box and she put a notice on her window: "If you need help, knock here." That is the Christian attitude to those around us.

36th Day: Tuesday of Holy Week

Luke 21:5–24

When some were speaking about the Temple, how it was adorned with lovely stones and offerings, Jesus said, "As for these things at which you are looking—days will come in which not one stone here will be left upon another, which will not be pulled down." They asked him, "Teacher, when, then, will these things be? And what will be the sign when these things are going to happen?" He said, "Take care that you are not led astray. Many will come in my name, saying, 'I am he!' and, 'The time is at hand!' Do not go after them. When you hear of wars and upheavals, do not be alarmed; for these things must happen first; but the end will not come at once."

Then he said to them, "Nation will rise against nation, and kingdom against kingdom. There will be great earthquakes; in some places there will be famines and pestilences; there will be terrifying things, and great signs from heaven. Before all these things, they will lay hands upon you, and they will hand you over to the synagogues and prisons, and you will be brought before kings and governors for the sake of my name. It will all be an opportunity for you to bear witness to me. So, then, make up your minds not to prepare your defence beforehand, for I will give you a mouth and wisdom against which all your opponents will be unable to stand or argue. You will be handed over even by parents, and brothers, and kinsfolk and friends; some of you will be put to death; and you will be hated by all for the sake of my name. But not one hair of your head will perish. By your endurance you will win your souls.

"When you shall see Jerusalem encircled by armies, then know that the time of the desolation is at hand. At that time let those in Jerusalem flee to the mountains; let those who are in the midst of her go out of her; and let not those in the country districts enter into her, because these are days of vengeance, to fulfil all that stands written. Woe to those who, in those days, are carrying a child in the womb, or who have a babe at the breast. For great distress will be upon the earth and wrath upon all the people. They shall fall by the edge of the sword, and they will be taken away captive to all nations. Jerusalem will be trodden underfoot by the Gentiles, until the times of Gentiles are completed."

From verse 5 onwards this becomes a very difficult chapter. Its difficulty rests in the fact that beneath it lie four different conceptions.

(i) There is the conception of "the day of the Lord." The Jews regarded time as being in two ages. There was "the present age," which was altogether bad and evil, incapable of being cured, and fit only for destruction. There was "the age to come," which was the golden age of God and of Jewish supremacy. But in between the two there would be "the day of the Lord," which would be a terrible time of cosmic upheaval and destruction, the desperate birth-pangs of the new age.

It would be a day of terror. "Behold the day of the Lord comes, cruel with wrath and fierce anger, to make the earth a desolation and to destroy its sinners from it" (Isaiah 13:9; cp. Joel 2:1, 2; Amos 5:18–20; Zephaniah 1:14–18). It would come suddenly. "The day of the Lord will come like a thief in the night" (1 Thessalonians 5:2; cp. 2 Peter 3:10). It would be a day when the world would be shattered. "The stars of the heavens and their constellations will not give their light; the sun will be dark at its rising and the moon will not shed its light. . . . Therefore I will make the heavens tremble, and the earth will be shaken out of its place, at the wrath of the Lord of hosts in the day of his fierce anger" (Isaiah 13:10–13; cp. Joel 2:30, 31; 2 Peter 3:10).

The day of the Lord was one of the basic conceptions of religious thought in the time of Jesus; everyone knew these terrible pictures. In this passage verses 9, 11, 25, 26 take their imagery from that.

(ii) There is the prophesied fall of Jerusalem. Jerusalem fell to the Roman armies in A.D. 70 after a desperate siege in which the inhabitants were actually reduced to cannibalism and in which the city had to be taken literally stone by stone. Josephus says that an incredible number of 1,100,000 people perished in the siege and 97,000 were carried away into captivity. The Jewish nation was obliterated; and the Temple was fired and became a desolation. In this passage verses 5, 6, 20–24 clearly refer to that event still to come.

(iii) There is the second coming of Christ. Jesus was sure that he was to come again and the early church waited for that coming. It will often help us to understand the New Testament passages about the second coming if we remember that much of the older imagery which had to do with the day of the Lord was taken and attached to it. In this passage verses 27 and 28 clearly refer to it. Before the second coming it was expected that many false claimants to be the Christ would arise and great upheavals take place. In this passage verses 7, 8, 9 refer to that.

(iv) There is the idea of persecution to come. Jesus clearly foresaw and foretold the terrible things his people would have to suffer for his sake in the days to come. In this passage verses 12–19 refer to that.

This passage will become much more intelligible and valuable if we remember that beneath it there is not one consistent idea, but these four allied conceptions.

37th Day: Wednesday of Holy Week

John 13:1–17

Before the Festival of the Passover, Jesus, in the knowledge that his hour had come to leave this world and to go to the Father, although he had always loved his own people in the world, decided to show them what his love was like in a way which went to the ultimate limit. The meal was in progress; and the devil had already put it into his heart that Judas Iscariot, the son of Simon, should betray him. Well knowing that the Father had given all things into his hands, and that he had come forth from God, and that he was going back to God, Jesus rose from the meal and laid aside his outer robe, and took a towel and put it round himself. Then he poured water into a ewer and began to wash the feet of his disciples and to wipe them with the towel which he had put round himself. He came to Simon Peter. Peter said to him: "Lord, are you going to wash my feet?" Jesus answered him: "You do not know now what I am doing, but you will understand afterwards." Peter said to him: "You will never wash my feet." Jesus answered him: "If I do not wash you, you have no part with me." Simon Peter said to him: "Lord, if that is so, do not wash my feet only, but my hands and my head too." Jesus said to him: "He who has been bathed has need only to have his feet washed. After that is done, he is altogether clean. And you are clean—but not all of you." He knew the one who was engineering his betrayal. That is why he said: "You are not all clean." So when he had washed their feet, and when he had taken his outer robe again, and when he had taken his place at table, he said to them: "Do you understand what I have done to you? You call me 'Teacher,' and you call me 'Lord.' And you are quite right to do so, for so I am. If then I, the Teacher and Lord, have washed your feet, so you ought to wash each other's feet, for I have given you an example, that, as I have done to you, you too should do to each other. This is the truth I tell you—the servant is not greater than his master, nor he who is sent greater than he who sent him. If you know these things you are blessed if you do them."

Few incidents in the Gospel story so reveal the character of Jesus and so perfectly show his love. When we think of what Jesus might have been and of what he might have done the supreme wonder of what he was and did comes home to us.

(i) Jesus knew all things had been given into his hands. He knew that his hour of humiliation was near, but he knew that his hour of glory was also near. Such a consciousness might well have filled him with pride; and yet, with the knowledge of the power and the glory that were his, he washed his disciples' feet. At that moment when he might have had supreme pride, he had supreme humility. Love is always like that. When, for example, someone falls ill, the person who loves him will perform the most menial services and delight to do them, because love is like that. Sometimes men feel that they are too distinguished to do the humble things, too important to do some menial task. Jesus was not so. He knew that he was Lord of all, and yet he washed his disciples' feet.

(ii) Jesus knew that he had come from God and that he was going to God. He might well have had a certain contempt for men and for the things of this world. He might well have thought that he was finished with the world now, for he was on the way to God. It was just at that time when God was nearest to him that Jesus went to the depths and the limits of his service. To wash the feet of the guests at a feast was the office of a slave. The disciples of the rabbis were supposed to render their masters personal service, but a service like this would never have been dreamed of. The wonderful thing about Jesus was that his nearness to God, so far from separating him from others, brought him nearer than ever to them.

There is more in the background of this passage than even John tells us. If we turn to Luke's account of the last meal together, we find the tragic sentence: "A dispute also arose among them, which of them was to be regarded as greatest" (Luke 22:24). Even within sight of the cross, the disciples were still arguing about matters of precedence and prestige.

It may well be that this very argument produced the situation which made Jesus act as he did. The roads of Palestine were unsurfaced and uncleaned. In dry weather they were inches deep in dust and in wet they were liquid mud. The shoes ordinary people wore were sandals, which were simply soles held on to the foot by a few straps. They gave little protection against the dust or the mud of the roads. For that reason there were always great waterpots at the door of a house; and a servant was there with a ewer and a towel to wash the soiled feet of the guests as they came in. Jesus' little company of friends had no servants. The duties which servants would carry out in wealthier circles they must have shared among each other. It may well be that on the night of this last meal together they had got themselves into such a state of competitive pride that not one of them would accept the duty of seeing that the water and the towels were there to wash the feet of the company as they came in; and Jesus mended their omission in the most vivid and dramatic way.

He himself did what none of them was prepared to do. Then he said: "You see what I have done. You call me your master and your Lord; and you are quite right; for so I am; and yet I am prepared to do this for you. Surely you don't think that a pupil deserves more honour than a teacher, or a servant than a master. Surely if I do this, you ought to be prepared to do it. I am giving you an example of how you ought to behave towards each other."

This ought to make us think. So often, even in churches, trouble arises because someone does not get his place. So often even ecclesiastical dignitaries are offended because they did not receive the precedence to which their office entitled them. Here is the lesson that there is only one kind of greatness, the greatness of service. The world is full of people who are standing on their dignity when they ought to be kneeling at the feet of their brethren. . . . When we are tempted to think of our dignity, our prestige, our rights, let us see again the picture of the Son of God, girt with a towel, kneeling at his disciples' feet.

38th Day: Maundy Thursday

John 18:1–11; 18:28–19:16

When Jesus had said these things he went out with his disciples across the Kedron Valley to a place where there was a garden, into which he and his disciples entered; and Judas, his betrayer, knew the place for Jesus often met with his disciples there. So Judas took a company of soldiers, together with officers from the chief priests and Pharisees, and went there with lanterns and torches and weapons. Jesus knew the things which were going to happen to him, so he came out and said: "Who are you looking for?" They answered: "Jesus of Nazareth." Jesus said to them: "I am he." And Judas, his betrayer, stood there with them. When he said to them: "I am he," they stepped back and fell on the ground. So Jesus again asked them: "Who are you looking for?" They said: "Jesus of Nazareth." Jesus said: "I told you that I am he. If it is I for whom you are looking, let these go, so that the word which scripture said may be fulfilled—I have lost none of those whom you gave me." Now Simon Peter had a sword and he drew it; and he struck the high priest's servant and cut off his right ear. The servant's name was Malchus. Jesus said to Peter: "Put your sword in its sheath. Shall I not drink the cup which my Father gave me?" . . .

They brought Jesus from Caiaphas to the governor's headquarters. It was early in the morning and they themselves did not enter into the headquarters, in case they should be defiled; but they wished to avoid defilement because they wished to eat the Passover. So Pilate came out to them and said: "What charge do you bring against this man?" They answered him: "If he had not been an evildoer, we would not have handed him over to you." Pilate said to them: "You take him, and judge him according to your laws." The Jews said to Pilate: "It is not permitted to us to put anyone to death." This happened that there might be fulfilled the word of Jesus, which he spoke in indication of the kind of death he was going to die. So Pilate went again into his headquarters, and called Jesus, and said to him: "Are you the King of the Jews?" Jesus answered: "Are you saying this because you have discovered it yourself? Or did others tell it to you about me?" Pilate answered: "Am I a Jew? Your own countrymen and the chief priests handed you over to me. What have you done?" Jesus answered: "My kingdom is not of this world. If my kingdom was of this world, my servants would have fought to prevent me being handed over to the Jews. But, as it is, my kingdom does not have its source here." So Pilate said to him: "So you are a king then?" Jesus said: "It is you who are saying that I am a king. The reason why I was born and came into the world is that I should bear witness to the truth. Every one who is of the truth hears my voice." "What is truth?" Pilate said to him.

When he had said this, he again went out to the Jews and said to them: "I find no fault in him. You have a custom that I should release one person to you at the Passover time. Do you wish me to release the King of the Jews for you?" They shouted: "Not this man, but Barabbas." And Barabbas was a brigand.

Then Pilate took Jesus and scourged him; and the soldiers plaited a crown of thorns, and put it on his head. And they put a purple robe on him; and they kept coming to him and saying: "Hail! King of the Jews!" And they dealt him repeated blows. Pilate came out again and said to them: "See! I bring him out to you, because I want you to know that I find no fault in him." So Jesus came out, wearing the crown of thorns and the purple robe. And Pilate said to them: "See! The Man!" So, when the chief priests and officers saw him, they shouted: "Crucify him! Crucify him!" Pilate said to them: "You take him, and crucify him! For I find no fault in him." The Jews answered him: "We have a law, and by that law he ought to die, because he made himself out to be the Son of God." When Pilate heard this saying, he was still more alarmed.

He went into his headquarters again, and said to Jesus: "Where do you come from?" Jesus gave him no answer. Pilate said to him: "Do you refuse to speak to me? Are you not aware that I have authority to release you, and authority to crucify you?" Jesus answered him: "You would have no authority against me whatsoever, unless it had been given to you from above. That is why he who betrayed me to you is guilty of the greater sin." From this moment Pilate tried every way to release him; but the Jews kept insistently shouting: "If you release this man, you are

not Caesar's friend. Every man who makes himself a king is an oppo-
nent of Caesar." So when Pilate heard these words, he brought Jesus out.
He took his seat on his judgment seat, in the place that is called the
Pavement—in Hebrew, Gabbatha. It was the day of the preparation
for the Passover. It was about twelve o'clock midday. He said to the Jews:
"See! Your king!" They shouted: "Away with him! Away with him! Cru-
cify him!" Pilate said to them: "Shall I crucify your king?" The chief
priests answered: "We have no king but Caesar." Then he handed him
over to them to be crucified.

This is the most dramatic account of the trial of Jesus in the New Testament, and to have cut it into small sections would have been to lose
the drama.

(i) First and foremost, no one can read this story without seeing
the sheer majesty of Jesus. There is no sense that he is on trial. When
a person faces him, it is not Jesus who is on trial; but the one who confronts him. Pilate may have treated many Jewish things with arrogant
contempt, but he did not so treat Jesus. We cannot help feeling that
it is Jesus who is in control and Pilate who is bewildered and floun-
dering in a situation which he cannot understand. The majesty of
Jesus never shone more radiantly than in the hour when he was on
trial.

(ii) Jesus speaks with utter directness to us of his kingdom; it is
not, he says, of this earth. The atmosphere in Jerusalem was always
explosive; during the Passover it was sheer dynamite. The Romans
well knew that, and during the Passover time they always drafted extra troops into Jerusalem. But Pilate never at any time had more than
three thousand soldiers under his command. Some would be in Caesarea, his headquarters; some would be on garrison duty in Samaria;
there cannot really have been more than a few hundred on duty in
Jerusalem. If Jesus had wished to raise the standard of rebellion and
to fight it out, he could have done it easily enough. But he makes it
quite clear that he claims to be a king and equally clear that his kingdom is not based on force but is a kingdom in the hearts of people.

He would never deny that he aimed at conquest, but it was the conquest of love.

(iii) Jesus tells us why he came into the world. He came to witness to the truth; he came to tell everyone the truth about God, the truth about themselves, and the truth about life. As Emerson had it:

> When half-gods go,
> The gods arrive.

The days of guessings and gropings and half-truths were gone. He came to tell the world the truth. That is one of the great reasons why we must either accept or refuse Christ. There is no half-way house about the truth. One either accepts it, or rejects it; and Christ is the truth.

(iv) We see the physical courage of Jesus. Pilate had him scourged. When criminals were scourged, they were tied to a whipping-post in such a way that their back was fully exposed. The lash was a long leathern thong, studded at intervals with pellets of lead and sharpened pieces of bone. It literally tore the person's back into strips. Few remained conscious throughout the ordeal; some died; and many went raving mad. Jesus stood that. And after it, Pilate led him out to the crowd and said: "See! The man!" Here is one of John's double meanings. It must have been Pilate's first intention to awaken the pity of the Jews. "Look!" he said. "Look at this poor, bruised, bleeding creature! Look at this wretchedness! Can you possibly wish to hound a creature like this to an utterly unnecessary death?" But we can almost hear the tone of his voice change as he says it, and see the wonder dawn in his eyes. And instead of saying it half-contemptuously, to awaken pity, he says it with an admiration that will not be repressed. The word that Pilate used is *ho anthropos,* which is the normal Greek for a human being; but not so long afterwards the Greek thinkers were using that very term for "the heavenly man," the ideal person, the pattern of humanity. It is always true that whatever else we say or do not say about Jesus, his sheer heroism is without parallel. Here indeed is a human being worthy of the name.

39th Day: Good Friday
John 19:17–22

So they took Jesus, and he, carrying his cross for himself, went out to the place that is called the Place of a Skull, which is called in Hebrew Golgotha. They crucified him there, and with him they crucified two others, one on either side, and Jesus in the middle. Pilate wrote a title, and put it on the cross. On it was written: "Jesus of Nazareth, the King of the Jews." Many of the Jews read this title, because the place where Jesus was crucified was near the city; and it was written in Hebrew, in Latin and in Greek. So the chief priests repeatedly said to Pilate: "Do not write, 'The King of the Jews.' But write, 'He said I am the King of the Jews.'" Pilate answered: "What I have written, I have written."

There was no more terrible death than death by crucifixion. Even the Romans themselves regarded it with a shudder of horror. Cicero declared that it was "the most cruel and horrifying death." Tacitus said that it was a "despicable death." It was originally a Persian method of execution. It may have been used because, to the Persians, the earth was sacred, and they wished to avoid defiling it with the body of an evil-doer. So they nailed him to a cross and left him to die there, looking to the vultures and the carrion crows to complete the work. The Carthaginians took over crucifixion from the Persians; and the Romans learned it from the Carthaginians.

Crucifixion was never used as a method of execution in the homeland, but only in the provinces, and there only in the case of slaves. It was unthinkable that a Roman citizen should die such a death. Cicero says: "It is a crime for a Roman citizen to be bound; it is a worse crime for him to be beaten; it is well nigh parricide for him to be killed; what am I to say if he be killed on a cross? A nefarious action such as that is incapable of description by any word, for there is none fit to describe it." It was that death, the most dreaded in the ancient world, the death of slaves and criminals, that Jesus died.

The routine of crucifixion was always the same. When the case had been heard and the criminal condemned, the judge uttered the fateful

sentence: "*Ibis ad crucem*," "You will go to the cross." The verdict was
carried out there and then. The condemned man was placed in the centre of a quaternion, a company of four Roman soldiers. His own cross
was placed upon his shoulders. Scourging always preceded crucifixion
and it is to be remembered how terrible scourging was. Often the criminal had to be lashed and goaded along the road, to keep him on his
feet, as he staggered to the place of crucifixion. Before him walked an
officer with a placard on which was written the crime for which he was
to die and he was led through as many streets as possible on the way to
execution. There was a double reason for that. There was the grim reason that as many as possible should see and take warning from his fate.
But there was a merciful reason. The placard was carried before the condemned man and the long route was chosen, so that if anyone could
still bear witness in his favour, he might come forward and do so. In
such a case, the procession was halted and the case retried.

In Jerusalem the place of execution was called "The Place of a
Skull," in Hebrew, *Golgotha*. (*Calvary* is the Latin for the Place of a
Skull.) It must have been outside the city walls, for it was not lawful
to crucify a person within the boundaries of the city. Where it was we
do not certainly know.

Luke 23:44–49

*By this time it was about midday, and there was darkness over the whole
land until 3 o'clock in the afternoon, and the light of the sun failed. And
the veil of the Temple was rent in the midst. When Jesus had cried with
a great voice, he said, "Father, into your hands I commend my spirit."
When he had said this he breathed his last. When the centurion saw what
had happened, he glorified God. "Truly," he said, "this was a good man."
All the crowds, who had come together to see the spectacle, when they saw
the things that had happened, went home beating their breasts. And all
his acquaintances, and the women who had accompanied him from
Galilee, stood far off and saw these things.*

Every sentence of this passage is rich in meaning.

(i) There was a great darkness as Jesus died. It was as if the sun
itself could not bear to look upon the deed human hands had

done. The world is ever dark in the day when people seek to banish Christ.

(ii) The Temple veil was rent in two. This was the veil which hid the Holy of Holies, the place where dwelt the very presence of God, the place where no one might ever enter except the High Priest, and he only once a year, on the great day of Atonement. It was as if the way to God's presence, hitherto barred, was thrown open to all. It was as if the heart of God, hitherto hidden, was laid bare. The birth, life and death of Jesus tore apart the veil which had concealed God from people. "He who has seen me," said Jesus, "has seen the Father" (John 14:9). On the cross, as never before and never again, we all have seen the love of God.

(iii) Jesus cried with a great voice. Three of the Gospels tell us of this great cry (cp. Matthew 27:50; Mark 15:37). John, on the other hand, does not mention the great cry but tells us that Jesus died saying, "It is finished" (John 19:30). In Greek and Aramaic "It is finished" is one word. "It is finished" and the great cry are, in fact, one and the same thing. Jesus died with a shout of triumph on his lips. He did not whisper, "It is finished," as one who is battered to his knees and forced to admit defeat. He shouted it like a victor who has won his last engagement with the enemy and brought a tremendous task to triumphant conclusion. "Finished!" was the cry of the Christ, crucified yet victorious.

(iv) Jesus died with a prayer on his lips. "Father, into your hands I commit my spirit." That is Psalm 31:5 with one word added—Father. That verse was the prayer every Jewish mother taught her child to say last thing at night. Just as we were taught, maybe, to say, "This night I lay me down to sleep," so the Jewish mother taught her child to say, before the threatening dark came down, "Into thy hands I commit my spirit." Jesus made it even more lovely for he began it with the word Father. Even on a cross Jesus died like a child falling asleep in his father's arms.

(v) The centurion and the crowd were deeply moved as Jesus died. His death did what even his life could not do; it broke hard hearts. Already Jesus' saying was coming true—"I, when I am lifted up from the earth, will draw all people to myself." The magnet of the cross had begun its work, even as he breathed his last.

John 19:38–42

After that, Joseph from Arimathaea, who because of fear of the Jews was a secret disciple of Jesus, asked Pilate to be allowed to take away Jesus' body, and Pilate gave him permission to do so. So he came and took his body away. Nicodemus, who first came to Jesus by night, came too, bringing a mixture of myrrh and aloes, about a hundred pounds in weight. So they took Jesus' body and they wrapped it in linen clothes with spices, as it is the Jewish custom to lay a body in the tomb. There was a garden in the place where he was crucified; and in the garden there was a new tomb in which no one had ever been laid. So they laid Jesus there, because it was the day of preparation for the Sabbath, because the tomb was near at hand.

So Jesus died, and what had to be done now must be done quickly, for the Sabbath was almost begun and on the Sabbath no work could be done. The friends of Jesus were poor and could not have given him a fitting burial; but two people came forward.

Joseph of Arimathaea was one. He had always been a disciple of Jesus; he was a great person and a member of the Sanhedrin, and up to now he had kept his discipleship secret for he was afraid to make it known. Nicodemus was the other. It was the Jewish custom to wrap the bodies of the dead in linen clothes and to put sweet spices between the folds of the linen. Nicodemus brought enough spices for the burial of a king. So Joseph gave to Jesus a tomb; and Nicodemus gave him the clothes to wear within the tomb.

There is both tragedy and glory here.

(i) There is tragedy. Both Nicodemus and Joseph were members of the Sanhedrin, but they were secret disciples of Jesus. Either they had absented themselves from the meeting of the Sanhedrin which examined him and formulated the charge against him, or they had sat silent through it all. What a difference it would have made to Jesus, if, among these condemning, hectoring voices, one voice had been raised in his support. What a difference it would have made to see loyalty on one face amidst that sea of bleak, envenomed faces. But Nicodemus and Joseph were afraid.

We so often leave our tributes until people are dead. How much greater would loyalty in life have been than a new tomb and a shroud fit for a king. One flower in life is worth all the wreaths in the world in death; one word of love and praise and thanks in life is worth all the panegyrics in the world when life is gone.

(ii) But there is glory here, too. The death of Jesus had done for Joseph and Nicodemus what not even his life could do. No sooner had Jesus died on the cross than Joseph forgot his fear and bearded the Roman governer with a request for the body. No sooner had Jesus died on the cross than Nicodemus was there to bring a tribute that all could see. The cowardice, the hesitation, the prudent concealment were gone. Those who had been afraid when Jesus was alive declared for him in a way that everyone could see as soon as he was dead. Jesus had not been dead an hour when his own prophecy came true: "I when I be lifted up from the earth will draw all people to myself" (John 12:32). It may be that the silence of Nicodemus or his absence from the Sanhedrin brought sorrow to Jesus; but it is certain that he knew of the way in which they cast their fear aside after the cross, and it is certain that already his heart was glad, for already the power of the cross had begun to operate, and already it was drawing men and women to him. The power of the cross was even then turning the coward into the hero, and the waverer into the one who took an irrevocable decision for Christ.

40th Day: Saturday of Holy Week

[*Editor's Note:* Scripture tells us little about what happened the day after Jesus' crucifixion. It was a Sabbath—by religious law and long custom, the activities of the disciples would have been at a minimum. But what of their thoughts and feelings? Jesus had said to the twelve, "Every one of you will be made to stumble because of me during this night; for it stands written, 'I will smite the shepherd, and the sheep of the flock shall be scattered abroad'"—and they had scattered in fear! He had told Peter, "During this night, before the cock crows, you will deny me three times"—and before morning, Peter had sworn three times that he didn't even know Jesus! Jesus had warned them, "This is the truth I tell you—one of you will betray me, one who is eating with me"—and Judas had hardened his heart and refused to give up the arrangements he already had made! Perhaps the day between Good Friday and Easter is the best time in the world to consider the "falling away" of all of Jesus' closest disciples.]

Luke 22:1–6

The Feast of Unleavened Bread, which is called the Passover, was near, and the chief priests and the scribes searched to find a way to destroy Jesus, for they were afraid of the people. And Satan entered into Judas, who was called Iscariot, who belonged to the number of the Twelve. So he went away and discussed with the chief priests and captains how he might betray Jesus to them. They were glad and they undertook to give him money. So he agreed, and he began to look for a suitable time to betray him, when the mob were not there.

Every male Jew, who was of age and who lived within 15 miles of the holy city, was bound by law to attend the Passover. But it was the ambition of every Jew in every part of the world (as it is still) to come to the Passover in Jerusalem at least once in a lifetime. To this day, when Jews keep the Passover in every land they pray that they may keep it next year in Jerusalem. Because of this vast numbers came to Jerusalem at the Passover time. Cestius was governor of Palestine in the time of Nero, and Nero tended to belittle the importance of the Jewish faith. To convince Nero of it, Cestius took a census of the lambs slain at one particular Passover. Josephus tells us that the number was 256,500. The law laid it down that the minimum number for a Passover celebration was 10. That means that on this occasion, if these figures are correct, there must have been more that 2,700,000 pilgrims to the Passover. It was in a city crowded like that that the drama of the last days of Jesus was played out.

The atmosphere of Passover time was always inflammable. The headquarters of the Roman government was at Caesarea, and normally only a small detachment of troops was stationed at Jerusalem; but for the Passover season many more were drafted in. The problem which faced the Jewish authorities was how to arrest Jesus without provoking a riot. It was solved for them by the treachery of Judas. Satan entered into Judas. Two things stand out.

(i) Just as God is ever looking for people to be his instruments, so is Satan. A person can be the instrument of good or of evil, of God or of the devil. The Zoroastrians see this whole universe as the battle ground between the god of the light and the god of the dark, and in that battle each person must choose a side. We, too, know that anyone can be the servant of the light, or of the dark.

(ii) But it remains true that Satan could not have entered into Judas unless Judas had opened the door. There is no handle on the outside of the door of the human heart. It must be opened from within.

It is our own decision whether we will choose to be the instrument of Satan or a weapon in the hand of God. We can enlist in either service. God help us choose aright!

Luke 22:31–38, 54–62

"Simon, Simon," Jesus said, "Look you, Satan has been allowed to have you that he may sift you like wheat. But I have prayed for you that your faith may not wholly fail. And you—when you have turned again— strengthen your brothers." He said to him, "Lord, I am ready to go with you to prison and to death." "Peter," he said, "I tell you, the cock will not crow today before you have three times denied that you know me." . . . So they seized Jesus and led him away, and brought him to the High Priest's house. Peter followed a long way away. When they had kindled a fire in the middle of the courtyard, and were sitting there together, Peter sat in the midst of them. A maidservant saw him as he sat in the firelight. She looked intently at him. "This man, too," she said, "was with him." He denied it. "Woman," he said, "I do not know him." Soon after another man saw him and said, "You, too, were one of them." Peter said, "Man, I am not!" About an hour elapsed and another insisted, "Truly this man, too, was with him. I know it for he is a Galilaean." Peter said, "Man, I don't know what you are talking about." And immediately—while he was still speaking—a cock crowed. And the Lord turned and looked at Peter. And Peter remem-

bered what the Lord had said, that he said to him, "Before the cock crows today you will deny me three times." And he went out and wept bitterly.

We take the story of the tragedy of Peter all in one piece. Peter was a strange paradoxical mixture.

(i) Even in spite of his denial he was fundamentally loyal. H. G. Wells once said, "A man may be a bad musician, and yet be passionately in love with music." No matter what Peter did, however terrible his failure, he was nonetheless passionately devoted to Jesus. There is hope for the person who, even while sinning, is still haunted by goodness.

(ii) Peter was well warned. Jesus warned him both directly and indirectly. Verses 33 to 38 with their talk of swords is a strange passage. But what they mean is this—Jesus was saying, "All the time so far you have had me with you. In a very short time you are going to be cast upon your own resources. What are you going to do about it? The danger in a very short time is not that you will possess nothing; but that you will have to fight for your very existence." This was not an incitement to armed force. It was simply a vivid eastern way of telling the disciples that their very lives were at stake. No one could say that the seriousness and danger of the situation, and his own liability to collapse were not presented to Peter.

(iii) Peter was over-confident. If a person says, "That is one thing I will never do," that is often the very thing that must be most carefully guarded against. Again and again castles have been captured because the attackers took the route which seemed unattackable and unscalable and at that very spot the defenders were off their guard. Satan is subtle. He attacks the point at which people are too sure of themselves, for there they are most likely to be unprepared.

(iv) In all fairness it is to be noted that Peter was one of the two disciples (John 18:15) who had the courage to follow Jesus into the courtyard of the High Priest's house at all. Peter fell to a temptation which could only have come to a brave person. The person of courage always runs more risks than the one who seeks a placid safety. Liability to temptation is the price that one pays to be adventurous in mind and in action. It may well be that it is better to fail in a gallant enterprise than to run away and not even to attempt it.

(v) Jesus did not speak to Peter in anger but looked at him in sorrow. Peter could have stood it if Jesus had turned and reviled him; but that voiceless, grief-laden look went to his heart like a sword and opened a fountain of tears.

> I think I'd sooner frizzle up,
> I' the flames of a burnin' 'ell,
> Than stand and look into 'is face,
> And 'ear 'is voice say—"Well?"

The penalty of sin is to face, not the anger of Jesus, but the heartbreak in his eyes.

(vi) Jesus said a very lovely thing to Peter. "When you have turned," he said, "strengthen your brothers." It is as if Jesus said to Peter, "You will deny me; and you will weep bitter tears; but the result will be that you will be better able to help your brothers who are going through it." We cannot really help others until we have been in the same furnace of affliction or the same abyss of shame as they have been. It was said of Jesus, "He can help others who are going through it because he has been through it himself" (Hebrews 2:18). To experience the shame of failure and disloyalty is not all loss, because it gives us a sympathy and an understanding that otherwise we would never have won.

Easter

Mark 16:1–8
When the Sabbath had passed, Mary of Magdala and Mary the mother of James and Salome bought spices to go and anoint his body. Very early in the morning on the first day of the week, when the sun was rising, they went to the tomb. They kept saying to each other, "Who will roll away the stone from the door of the tomb for us?" They looked up and they saw that the stone had been rolled away, for it was very large. And they went into the tomb, and they saw a young man sitting on the right side, clothed in

a long, white robe. They were utterly amazed. He said to them, "Do not be amazed. You are looking for Jesus of Nazareth who was crucified. He is risen. He is not here. See! There is the place where they laid him. But go! Tell his disciples and Peter, 'He goes before you into Galilee. There you will see him as he told you.' " And they went out and fled from the tomb, for fear and astonishment gripped them. And they told no one anything for they were afraid.

There had not been time to render the last services to the body of Jesus. The Sabbath had intervened and the women who wished to anoint the body had not been able to do so. As early as possible after the Sabbath had passed, they set out to perform this sad task.

They were worried about one thing. Tombs had no doors. When the word door is mentioned it really means opening. In front of the opening was a groove, and in the groove ran a circular stone as big as a cart-wheel; and the women knew that it was quite beyond their strength to move a stone like that. But when they reached the tomb, the stone was rolled away, and inside was a messenger who gave them the unbelievable news that Jesus had risen from the dead.

One thing is certain—if Jesus had not risen from the dead, we would never have heard of him. The attitude of the women was that they had come to pay the last tribute to a dead body. The attitude of the disciples was that everything had finished in tragedy. By far the best proof of the Resurrection is the existence of the Christian church. Nothing else could have changed sad and despairing men and women into people radiant with joy and flaming with courage. The Resurrection is the central fact of the whole Christian faith. Because we believe in the Resurrection certain things follow.

(i) Jesus is not a figure in a book but a living presence. It is not enough to study the story of Jesus like the life of any other great historical figure. We may begin that way but we must end by meeting him.

(ii) Jesus is not a memory but a presence. The dearest memory fades. The Greeks had a word to describe time meaning "time which wipes all things out." Long since, time would have wiped out the memory of Jesus unless he had been a living presence forever with us.

And warm, sweet, tender, even yet
A present help is he;
And faith has still its Olivet,
And love its Galilee.

Jesus is not someone to discuss so much as someone to meet.

(iii) The Christian life is not the life of a person who knows about Jesus, but the life of one who knows Jesus. There is all the difference in the world between knowing about someone and knowing that person. Most people know about Queen Elizabeth or the President of the United States but not so many know them. The greatest scholar in the world who knows everything about Jesus is less than the humblest Christian who knows him.

(iv) There is an endless quality about the Christian faith. It should never stand still. Because our Lord is a living Lord there are new wonders and new truths waiting to be discovered all the time.

But the most precious thing in this passage is in two words which are in no other Gospel. "Go," said the messenger. "Tell his disciples and Peter." How that message must have cheered Peter's heart when he received it! He must have been tortured with the memory of his disloyalty, and suddenly there came a special message for him. It was characteristic of Jesus that he thought, not of the wrong Peter had done him but of the remorse he was undergoing. Jesus was far more eager to comfort the penitent sinner than to punish the sin. Someone has said, "The most precious thing about Jesus is the way in which he trusts us on the field of our defeat."

John 20:11–18

But Mary stood weeping outside at the tomb. As she wept she stooped down, and looked into the tomb, and she saw two angels sitting there in white robes, one at the head, and the other at the feet of the place where Jesus' body had been lying. They said to her: "Woman, why are you crying?" She said to them: "Because they have taken my Lord away, and I do not know where they have laid him." When she had said this, she turned round, and saw Jesus standing there, and did not know that it was Jesus. Jesus said to her: "Woman, why are you crying? Who are you look-

*ing for?" She, thinking that he was the gardener, said to him: "Sir, if you
are the man who has removed him, tell me where you have laid him, and
I will take him away." Jesus said to her: "Mary!" She turned, and said to
him in Hebrew, "Rabbouni!" which means, "Master!" Jesus said to her:
"Do not touch me! For I have not yet ascended to the Father. But go to
my brethren, and say to them that I am going to ascend to my Father and
your Father, to my God and your God." Mary of Magdala came to the
disciples, telling them: "I have seen the Lord," and telling them what he
had said to her.*

Someone has called this story the greatest recognition scene in all lit-
erature. To Mary belongs the glory of being the first person to see the
Risen Christ. The whole story is scattered with indications of her love.
She had come back to the tomb; she had taken her message to Peter
and John, and then must have been left behind in their race to the
tomb so that by the time she got there, they were gone. So she stood
there weeping. There is no need to seek for elaborate reasons why
Mary did not know Jesus. The simple and the poignant fact is that
she could not see him through her tears.

Whatever happened, Jesus sent Mary back to the disciples with the
message that what he had so often told them was now about to happen—he was on his way to his father; and Mary came with the news,
"I have seen the Lord."

In that message of Mary there is the very essence of Christianity,
for a Christian is essentially one who can say: "I have seen the Lord."
Christianity does not mean knowing about Jesus; it means knowing
him. It does not mean arguing about him; it means meeting him. It
means the certainty of experience that Jesus is alive.

Monday after Easter

Luke 24:13–35

*Now—look you—on that same day two of them were on the way to a vil-
lage called Emmaus, which is about seven miles from Jerusalem; and they
talked with each other about all the things which had happened. As they
talked about them, and discussed them, Jesus himself came up to them and*

joined them on their way. But their eyes were fastened so that they did not recognize him. He said to them, "What words are these that you are exchanging with each other as you walk?" And they stood with faces twisted with grief. One of them, called Cleopas, answered, "Are you the only visitor in Jerusalem who does not know the things that happened in it in these days?" "What kind of things?" he said to them. They said to him, "The story of Jesus of Nazareth, who was a prophet mighty in deed and in word before God and all the people; and how our chief priests and rulers handed him over to sentence of death and how they crucified him. As for us—we were hoping that he was the one who was going to rescue Israel. Yes—and to add to it all—this is the third day since these things happened. Yes and some women of our number astonished us, for they went early to the tomb, and, when they did not find his body, they came saying that they had seen a vision of angels, who said that he was alive. And some of our company went to the tomb and found it just as the women had said—but they did not see him." He said to them, "O foolish ones and slow in heart to believe in all the things that the prophets said! Was it not necessary that the anointed one should suffer and enter into his glory?" And beginning from Moses and all the prophets, he expounded to them the things concerning himself in all the scriptures. As they came near the village to which they were going, he made as if he would have gone on; and they pressed him. "Stay with us," they said, "because it is towards evening, and the day is already far spent." So he came in to stay with them. When he had taken his place at table with them, he took bread, and blessed it and broke it, and gave it to them; and their eyes were opened and they recognized him; and he vanished out of their sight. They said to each other, "Was not our heart burning within us while he was talking to us on the road, as he opened the scriptures to us?" And they arose that very hour and went back to Jerusalem and found the eleven gathered together and those with them, and found that they were saying, "It is a fact that the Lord has risen, and he has appeared to Simon." So they recounted all that had happened on the road, and how he was known to them in the breaking of bread.

This is another of the immortal short stories of the world.

(i) It tells of two men who were walking towards the sunset. It has been suggested that that is the very reason why they did not recognize Jesus. Emmaus was west of Jerusalem. The sun was sinking, and the setting sun so dazzled them that they did not know their Lord. However that may be, it is true that the Christian is one who walks not towards the sunset but towards the sunrise. Long ago it was said to the children of Israel that they journeyed in the wilderness towards the sunrising (Numbers 21:11). The Christian goes onwards, not to a night which falls, but to a dawn which breaks—and that is what, in their sorrow and their disappointment, the two on the Emmaus road had not realized.

(ii) It tells us of the ability of Jesus to make sense of things. The whole situation seemed to these two men to have no explanation. Their hopes and dreams were shattered. There is all the poignant, wistful, bewildered regret in the world in their sorrowing words, "We were hoping that he was the one who was going to rescue Israel." They were the words of men whose hopes were dead and buried. Then Jesus came and talked with them, and the meaning of life became clear and the darkness became light. A story-teller makes one character say to another with whom he has fallen in love, "I never knew what life meant until I saw it in your eyes." It is only in Jesus that, even in the bewildering times, we learn what life means.

(iii) It tells us of the courtesy of Jesus. He made as if he would have gone on. He would not force himself upon them; he awaited their invitation to come in. God gave to humankind the greatest and the most perilous gift in the world, the gift of free-will; we can use it to invite Christ to enter our lives or to allow him to pass on.

(iv) It tells how he was known to them in the breaking of bread. This always sounds a little as if it meant the sacrament; but it does not. It was at an ordinary meal in an ordinary house, when an ordinary loaf was being divided, that these two recognized Jesus. It has been beautifully suggested that perhaps they were present at the feeding of the five thousand, and, as he broke the bread in their cottage home, they recognized his hands again. It is not only at the communion table we can be with Christ; we can be with him at the dinner table too. He is not only the host in his church; he is the guest in every home.

(v) It tells how these two men, when they received such great joy, hastened to share it. It was a seven miles' tramp back to Jerusalem, but they could not keep the good news to themselves. The Christian message is never fully ours until we have shared it with someone else.

(vi) It tells how, when they reached Jerusalem, they found others who had already shared their experience. It is the glory of Christians that we live in a fellowship of people who have had the same experience as we have had. It has been said that true friendship begins only when people share a common memory and can say to each other, "Do you remember?" Each of us is one of a great fellowship of people who share a common experience and a common memory of their Lord.

(vii) It tells that Jesus appeared to Peter. That must remain one of the great untold stories of the world. But surely it is a lovely thing that Jesus should make one of his first appearances to one who had denied him. It is the glory of Jesus that he can give self-respect back to the penitent sinner.

John 20:24–29

But Thomas, who is called Didymus, one of the Twelve, was not with them when Jesus came. The other disciples told him: "We have seen the Lord." He said to them: "Unless I see the print of the nails in his hands, and put my finger in the print of the nails, and unless I put my hand into his side, I will not believe." Eight days later the disciples were again in the room, and Thomas was with them. When the doors were locked, Jesus came and stood in the midst of them, and said: "Peace be to you." Then he said to Thomas: "Stretch out your finger here, and look at my hands; stretch out your hand and put it into my side; and show yourself not faithless but believing." Thomas answered: "My Lord and my God!" Jesus said to him: "You have believed because you have seen me. Blessed are those who have not seen and who have believed."

To Thomas the cross was only what he had expected. When Jesus had proposed going to Bethany, after the news of Lazarus's illness had come, Thomas's reaction had been: "Let us also go, that we may die with him" (John 11:16). Thomas never lacked courage, but he was the natural pessimist. There can never be any doubt that he loved

Jesus. He loved him enough to be willing to go to Jerusalem and die with him when the other disciples were hesitant and afraid. What he had expected had happened, and when it came, for all that he had expected it, he was broken-hearted, so broken-hearted that he could not meet the eyes of men, but must be alone with his grief. . . . So it happened that, when Jesus came back again, Thomas was not there; and the news that he had come back seemed to him far too good to be true, and he refused to believe it. Belligerent in his pessimism, he said that he would never believe that Jesus had risen from the dead until he had seen and handled the print of the nails in his hands and thrust his hand into the wound the spear had made in Jesus' side. (There is no mention of any wound-print in Jesus' feet because in crucifixion the feet were usually not nailed, but only loosely bound to the cross.)

Another week elapsed and Jesus came back again; and this time Thomas was there. And Jesus knew Thomas's heart. He repeated Thomas's own words, and invited him to make the test that he had demanded. And Thomas's heart ran out in love and devotion, and all he could say was: "My Lord and my God!" Jesus said to him: "Thomas, you needed the eyes of sight to make you believe; but the days will come when others will see with the eye of faith and believe." The character of Thomas stands out clear before us.

(i) He made one mistake. He withdrew from the Christian fellowship. He sought loneliness rather than togetherness. And because he was not there with his fellow Christians he missed the first coming of Jesus. We miss a great deal when we separate ourselves from the Christian fellowship and try to be alone. Things can happen to us within the fellowship of Christ's church which will not happen when we are alone. When sorrow comes and sadness envelops us, we often tend to shut ourselves up and refuse to meet people. That is the very time when, in spite of our sorrow, we should seek the fellowship of Christ's people, for it is there that we are likeliest of all to meet him face to face.

(ii) But Thomas had two great virtues. He absolutely refused to say that he understood what he did not understand, or that he believed what he did not believe. There is an uncompromising honesty about him. He would never still his doubts by pretending that they did not exist. He was not the kind who would rattle off a creed without understanding what it was all about. Thomas had to be sure—and he was quite right. Tennyson wrote:

There lives more faith in honest doubt,
Believe me, than in half the creeds.

There is more ultimate faith in the person who insists on being sure than in the one who glibly repeats things never thought out, and which may not really be believed. It is doubting like that which in the end arrives at certainty.

(ii) Thomas's other great virtue was that when he was sure, he went the whole way. "My Lord and my God!" said he. There was no halfway house about Thomas. He was not airing his doubts just for the sake of mental acrobatics; he doubted in order to become sure; and when he did, his surrender to certainty was complete. And a person who fights through doubts to the conviction that Jesus Christ is Lord has attained to a certainty that one who unthinkingly accepts things can never reach.

Tuesday after Easter

Matthew 28:16–20
So the eleven disciples went into Galilee, to the mountain where Jesus had instructed them to go. And they saw him and worshipped him; but some were not sure. Jesus came and spoke to them. "All power," he said, "is given to me in heaven and upon earth. Go, therefore, and make all nations my disciples, baptizing them in the name of the Father and of the Son and of the Holy Spirit, and teaching them to keep all the commandments I have given you. And, look you, I am with you throughout all days until the end of the world."

Here we come to the end of the Gospel story; here we listen to the last words of Jesus to his disciples; and in this last meeting Jesus did three things.

(i) He assured them of his power. Surely nothing was outside the power of him who had died and conquered death. Now they were the servants of a Master whose authority upon earth and in heaven was beyond all question.

(ii) He gave them a commission. He sent them out to make all the world his disciples. It may well be that the instruction to baptize is something which is a development of the actual words of Jesus. That may be argued about; the salient fact remains that the commission of Jesus is to win all persons for himself.

(iii) He promised them a presence. It must have been a staggering thing for eleven humble Galilaeans to be sent forth to the conquest of the world. Even as they heard it, their hearts must have failed them. But, no sooner was the command given, than the promise followed. They were sent out—as we are—on the greatest task in history, but with them there was the greatest presence in the world.

> Though few and small and weak your bands,
> Strong in your Captain's strength,
> Go to the conquest of all lands;
> All must be his at length.

Luke 24:50–53

Jesus led them out as far as Bethany; and he raised his hands and blessed them; and as he was blessing them he parted from them, and was borne up into heaven. And when they had worshipped him they returned to Jerusalem with great joy; and they were continually in the Temple praising God.

The ascension must always remain a mystery, for it attempts to put into words what is beyond words and to describe what is beyond description. But that something such should happen was essential. It was unthinkable that the appearances of Jesus should grow fewer and fewer until finally they petered out. That would have wrecked the faith. There had to come a day of dividing when the Jesus of earth finally became the Christ of heaven. But to the disciples the ascension was obviously three things.

(i) It was an ending. The days when their faith was faith in a flesh and blood person and depended on his flesh and blood presence were over. Now they were linked to someone who was forever independent of space and time.

(ii) Equally it was a beginning. The disciples did not leave the scene heart-broken; they left it with great joy, because now they knew that they had a Master from whom nothing could separate them any more.

> I know not where his islands lift
> Their fronded palms in air;
> I only know I cannot drift
> Beyond his love and care.

"I am sure," said Paul, "that nothing—nothing in life or death—can separate us from the love of God in Christ Jesus our Lord" (Romans 8:38, 39).

(iii) Further, the ascension gave the disciples the certainty that they had a friend, not only on earth, but in heaven. Surely it is the most precious thing of all to know that in heaven there awaits us that self-same Jesus who on earth was wondrous kind. To die is not to go out into the dark; it is to go to him.

So they went back to Jerusalem, and they were continually in the Temple praising God. It is not by accident that Luke's Gospel ends where it began—in the house of God.

John 20:30, 31

Jesus did many other signs in the presence of his disciples which have not been written in this book. These have been written that you may believe that Jesus is the Anointed One, the Son of God, and that believing you may have life in his name.

It is quite clear that as the Gospel was originally planned, it comes to an end with this verse. Chapter 21 is to be regarded as an appendix and an afterthought.

No passage in the Gospels better sums up the aim of the writers than this.

(i) It is quite clear that the Gospels never set out to give a full account of the life of Jesus. They do not follow him from day to day but are selective. They give us, not an exhaustive account of everything that Jesus said or did, but a selection which shows what he was like and the kind of things he was always doing.

(ii) It is also clear that the Gospels were not meant to be biographies of Jesus, but appeals to take him as Saviour, Master and Lord. Their aim was, not to give information, but to give life. It was to paint such a picture of Jesus that the reader would be bound to see that the person who could speak and teach and act and heal like this could be none other than the Son of God; and that in that belief he might find the secret of real life.

When we approach the Gospels as history and biography, we approach them in the wrong spirit. We must read them, not primarily as historians seeking information, but as men and women seeking God.